MYTHOLOGY TRILOGY

A Concise Guide to Greek, Norse and Egyptian Mythology

Table of Contents

EGYPTIAN MYTHOLOGY

GREEK MYTHOLOGY

*A Concise Guide to Ancient Gods, Heroes,
Beliefs and Myths*

Copyright © 2016 by Hourly History

Introduction

"Man: a being in search of meaning."

—Plato; a philosopher c428-348BCE

If you look back on the events of your day today, I am prepared to guess that you referenced Greek mythology at least twice, if not three times. Perhaps you are laughing, but think back: did you look at your horoscope under your sign of the *Zodiac*? Did you work like a *Spartan* to catch up on some work? Was your PC at work attacked by a *Trojan* virus? Did you order something via *Amazon.com*? Did you buy some household shopping at lunch time and pick up a bottle of *Ajax*? Perhaps you found a second-hand copy of *"The Tanglewood Tales"* by Nigel Hawthorne for your niece's birthday while you were out booking tickets to go to *"Orpheus in the Underworld"* on Saturday. Afterwards, you might have wondered what it would be like to be *"as rich as Croesus"*! Television news channels today are discussing whether China and the United States are going to fall into the *Thucydides' Trap* - Thucydides being a famous Greek military leader who wrote about "the likelihood of conflict between a rising power and a currently dominant one."

All the many ancient civilizations that have come before us have left traces of the mythologies that guided them - but none more so than the Greeks. In common with other mythologies, early Greek mythology was handed down through the oral tradition of travelling bards from Minoa, Mycenae and Mesopotamia, re-telling tales that go back as far as 2700 BCE, like the epic of Gilgamesh, the semi-mythic King of Uruk. The Greeks also have one of the most complicated mythological systems, rife with some anomalies as well. While it's not perhaps the oldest, running from approximately 2000 BCE till the end of the Hellenistic era around c146 BCE, it is well-documented nevertheless. We know a great deal about it mostly through ancient pottery of all things; the ancient Egyptians may have inscribed their beliefs on the interior walls of their incredible burial sites. But the customs of the Greeks survived best on bits of decorated pottery in the form of vases, urns and pots that have defied the ravages of eons. Pottery survived, sometimes even intact, better than built structures and paintings, and these objects were decorated with abstract designs as well as realistic depictions of everyday life. The best-known style was the silhouetted, black figures in action, for example a vase by the potter Exekias depicting Achilles killing the Amazon Penthesilia dated 540 BCE.

What was different about Greek mythology though was the emphasis on the written record. This was a result of an unusual leaning towards the dramatic arts of rhetoric, poetics and theatrical performances as well as gifted historians like Herodotus (484–425 BCE) and Thucydides (460-395 BCE). Our ancestors have always endeavoured to keep records of events, for example the so-called *Doomsday Book*, but the Greeks were the first important civilization to translate these lists of happenings into written history with a narrative attached – often dramatized – which allows us to witness our past today. The fact that so much Greek custom and culture was subsumed in the wave of Roman influence as the Roman Empire advanced across the ancient world has had the odd effect of highlighting many aspects of Grecian life instead of obliterating it. One just has to remember the Roman aristocrat Publius Ovidius Naso (43 BCE–17 CE) to appreciate this. He is better remembered as Ovid, the poet who based his work on Greek and Roman mythology. His *Metamorphosis* would become one of Shakespeare's most fruitful story sources. This brief guide will cover the rise of Greece and biographies of selected gods from its colourful pantheon. I will touch on the ways Greek mythology is different from other popular mythologies and recount some key aspects of their beliefs. The adventures, triumphs and sorrows of their heroes and heroines are told in dramatic plays that still grip modern audiences today. This is as a result of one of the most interesting gods of all times; Dionysus, twice-born son of the great Zeus.

Ulysses

Myth is the nothing that is all
The very sun that breaks through the skies
Is a bright and speechless myth-
God's dead body,
Naked and alive.

This hero who cast anchor here,
Because he never was, slowly came to exist.
Without ever being, he sufficed us.
Having never come here,
He came to be our founder.

Thus the legend, little by little,
Seeps into reality
And constantly enriches it.
Life down below, half
Of nothing, perishes.

—Fernando Pessoa 1888-1935

Chapter One

What Is A Myth?

And why do we have them anyway? There are many definitions according to scholars:*"Myth is a traditional tale with secondary, partial reference to something of collective importance,"* according to Walter Burkert. *"A myth is a socially traditional story,"* according to Stephen Kershaw. Notice that neither scholar mentions "truth." Even so, it is a mistake to equate a myth with a "lie" or an untruth. Remember that we look back on ancient times and think about myths as stories or beliefs, but in the time of our ancestors the "myth" was their reality. So why were they constructed? The general consensus is that we created myths to explain our environment to ourselves and to make sense of our experiences, to answer the question about where we came from, who we are and how we can be happy. One can think of mythology as the forerunner of what we came to call philosophy, which is why myths are so entangled with religion and existentialism - and why they are so important. Myths are also how we recall historical events. It is incredible to think of all the history of the ancient world held in so fragile a vessel as the human mind!

Greece is located in southern Europe and is a peninsula and a surrounding archipelago enclosed on three sides by the Ionian, Aegean and Mediterranean Seas. Indo-European people, Minoan and Mycenaean, migrated into the area from c2000 BCE, settling successfully on the mainland and scattered islands. The legendary King Minos built a magnificent palace at Knossos on Crete, which grew to become the center of the Minoan Empire. The settlers were mainly pastoral farmers and crop growers who were organized into immensely independent and resourceful groups of families. The progress of these family groups was disrupted by a Dorian invasion, bringing a dark age to the region for nearly 500 years until the emergence of what would be a celebrated time of highly civilized city-states known as the Classical period, which ended in c336 BCE. The exploits of Alexander the Great as he set about conquering the world disrupted Greece and Thebes fell to him in c335 BCE, marking the start of the Hellenistic period lasting until c146 BCE.

It is virtually impossible to estimate the Greek population during this historic period. The best guess for the 5th century BCE is anywhere between 800,000 to 3 million people. What is certain though is that ancient Greece is regarded as the cradle of mankind in terms of art, culture and democracy - and that is why there is still an intense interest in the mythology of these times.

*"Bury my body and don't build any monument.
Keep my hands out so the people know the one who won
the world
had nothing in hand when he died."*

—Alexander the Great 356–323BCE

Chapter Two

The Sources Of Greek Mythology

The Greeks were polytheistic and as a result of the extensive and varied geographical nature of the burgeoning civilization, the myths that evolved included many variations–even more than usually expected in an oral tradition. There was no *one* sacred text to follow and no formal religious or social structure – each little settlement or village had their own favorite gods, and sometimes there were conflicting interpretations of popular myths. Mythography was certainly taught at schools, and by 500 BCE there were "handbooks" of myths collected by various people. There are several ancient texts which are pivotal to our understanding of this time. One of the most important, *"The Iliad"*, is an epic poem written in 750 BCE by Homer. It recounts the story of the end of the Trojan War and is one of the major sources for our understanding of the times. Homer's other great work. *"The Odyssey."* takes place after the fall of Troy and tells the story of Odysseus' fantastic voyage home to his wife Penelope. Incredibly these magnificent sources have come down to us in their entirety. Hesiod, a contemporary of Homer and a fellow poet, he presents an incredibly detailed genealogy of the gods from Khaos to Polydoros in "Theogony", which features a vivid description of the creation of the universe as well as the events of the war with the Titans. A second work by Hesiod, *"Works and Days"*, covers human life and moral values through stories of well-known mythical figures like Prometheus and Pandora, offers advice on farming, and explains lucky days and unlucky days.

Lyric poetry was also abundant during this time. A poem like *"He is more than a hero"* by Sappho (c610–c570 BCE) captures the personal nature of the "myths" and the ambivalent sexuality that formed part of Grecian life.

He is more than a hero
he is a god in my eyes—
the man who is allowed
to sit beside you –

he who listens intimately
to the sweet murmur of
your voice, the enticing

laughter that makes my own
heart beat fast. If I meet
you suddenly, I can't

speak — my tongue is broken;
a thin flame runs under
my skin; seeing nothing,

hearing only my own ears

drumming, I drip with sweat;
trembling shakes my body

and I turn paler than
dry grass. At such times
death isn't far from me.

Pindar (c522–c438 BCE) was probably the greatest lyrical poet and specialized in large-scale choral odes often celebrating Olympian athletic victories. He was also known to have "corrected" written copies of traditional mythology.

Apollonius of Rhodes was probably born somewhere in the first half of the third century BCE and supplies an excellent source on the myth of Jason and the Golden Fleece in his work *Argonautica*. He is sometimes mistaken for the erudite Grecian scholar, Apollodorus, who was born in c130 BCE and is best known for his "*Chronicle of Greek History.*"

The philosophers of the Classical Period also supply some information on the mythography of Greece albeit, more negative information than positive. Socrates (c469–399 BCE) is said to be the father of philosophy, a controversial figure in Greek history, he was a gifted teacher. His pedagogical style was to ask questions of his pupils and use their answers to improve their way of reasoning – a style still used today that bears his name, as it's commonly referred to as the Socratic Method. He was critical of the gods and went as far as to suggest that there might actually only *be* one god. When he heard that the Oracle at Delphi had apparently said he was the wisest man alive, Socrates was quite upset. One of the quotes attributed to him was: *"I can't teach anybody anything; I can only make them think."* Socrates' greatest pupil, Plato (429-347 BCE) was openly scathing of Homer and Hesiod: *"These, methinks, composed false stories which they told and still tell to mankind."* Aristotle (384-322 BCE) too was fairly dismissive of the school of Hesiod, saying *"about those who have invented clever mythologies it is not worthwhile to take a serious book."* It is therefore somewhat confusing to find that he wrote an entire book on the subject called *"Metaphysics,"* in which he expressed appreciation for the fact that great myths would often form the basis of philosophical formulations about the nature of being . *"It is the mark of an educated mind to be able to entertain a thought without accepting it,"* said Aristotle.

However, the most important source of information about the nature and place of Greek myths is however the work of the great dramatists of the Classical Age: Aeschylus, Sophocles, Euripides and Aristophanes. They deserve a much more in-depth look – more on them later.

"It lies in the lap of the gods."

—Homer

Chapter Three

The Creation Of The Universe And The Gods

The beginning of time is very murky in Greek mythology, with many variations of what is supposed to have happened, especially in the order of events. Rather than get bogged down in detail I have chosen to steer a middle path informed by hours of reading on the subject. In the beginning there was Khaos, was either a god itself *or* a set of circumstances. Our word "chaos" comes from this word. But in the tale of early Greek mythology it has a very different meaning: *a state of utter confusion or disorder; a total lack of organization or order.* In Greek mythology it was a "formless or void" state and has nothing to do with a great deal of noise and confusion. It was actually a gap or a space that existed, perhaps as a result of the separation of heaven and earth. From the depth of Khaos came Gaia i.e. the earth itself. Gaia was beautiful; she separated heaven from earth, water from land and air from space. She gave birth to Uranus (the sky) who in turn created rain to fashion the mountains, the rivers, the animals and the plants. Gaia also gave rise to Nyx (night), Pontus (the sea), Tartarus (the Underworld) and Erebus, the darkness that covers the Underworld. In some versions Gaia also gives birth to the goddess Aphrodite, who brings love and beauty into the world.

Gaia and Uranus mate to create their first of many children, the 12 Titans – huge and powerful gods, like Oceanus, who has thousands of children i.e. all the rivers of the world. Another Titian, Hyperion, is credited with the creation of Dawn, the Sun and the Moon. Significant of their offspring was Cronus, who will soon play a pivotal and painful part in this epic story. The second set of gods born from Gaia and Uranus are the Cyclopes; they are also huge and powerful and were the first blacksmiths. The three Cyclopes were known as Steropes, Brontes and Argus. Each had one fearful eye in the middle of his forehead and they were responsible for lightning, lightning bolts and thunder. The world was steadily becoming noisier. Uranus and Gaia had three more formidable children known as the Hecatoncheirs – each had a hundred hands and fifty heads and they were gigantic enough to hurl mountains around. Appropriately, they were in charge of earthquakes.

Uranus was actually a reasonable leader, and all the gods were fairly happy under his rule. However, Uranus himself developed an intense dislike of his own offspring which is not really explained in any way. He decided to stop his children from being and he shoved them unceremoniously back into Gaia's womb, interpreted as "hidden in secret parts of the earth." This infuriated her, and when her pleadings with him to relieve her of this pain and burden had no effect, she plotted with Cronus, one of her offspring, to punish Uranus for this cruelty. The plan was devilish. When next Uranus came to lie with her, Cronus, presumably from inside his mother, cut off his father's genitals with a scythe and cast them, bleeding, onto the earth. *"And not vainly did they fall from his hand; for all the bloody drops that gushed forth Gaia received, and as the seasons moved round she bore the strong Erinyes and the great Gigantes...with gleaming armour, holding long spears in their hands and the Nymphai whom they call Meliai all over the boundless earth."* (Theogony by Hesiod) The Erinyes were the Fates or Furies, including gods like Poinai, Aroi and Praxidikai, whose three respective purviews were Retaliations, Curses and Exacting Justice. The Gigantes were a tribe of very strong giants and the cause of thermal activity and volcanoes. They included gods like Enkelades and Porphyrian. The Meliai were the honey-nurse nymphs of the god Zeus and perhaps even the nurses of mankind. In some versions the genitals are cast into the sea and Aphrodite, the goddess of love, is born from the foam that arises from the semen.

This would not be the only time a son usurps his father. A triumphant Cronus becomes king of the gods, frees all his siblings and marries Rhea. his sister. They produce six children; the gods Hestia, Demeter, Hera, Hades, Poseidon and Zeus. Somehow Cronus becomes aware of a prophecy that he will be unseated by one of his children, so each time one is born he swallows them alive. Rhea is desperate to save at least one of her children, and when Zeus is born she secretly sends him away to Crete to be brought up by nymphs. In his place, she wraps a large stone in swaddling clothes and hands it to Cronus, who promptly swallows it down.

Zeus grows up into a formidable warrior and lover and returns to Olympus as a cup bearer to Cronus. This allows him to slip Cronus the proverbial "Mickey Finn," a magic potion which causes him to regurgitate Zeus' siblings (as well as the rock representing Zeus). This rock, known as an omphalos stone, is enshrined at the Delphi Shrine to this day; while there are several explanations for this stone coming to reside at Delphi, this is but one of them.

In gratitude his siblings joined forces with Zeus against their father. This set up a simmering rivalry between the Olympian gods led by Zeus and the Titans led by Cronus. The resulting conflict is known as the Titanomachy, which lasted ten years. Eventually Zeus prevailed and the defeated Titans were banished to Tartarus with but a few exceptions. The Titan Atlas was tasked with holding the earth up safely on his shoulders; the Titan brothers Epimetheus and Prometheus, who had sided with Zeus, were tasked with creating the first mortal men instead of being banished.

The victorious Olympians retired to Mount Olympus and looked forward to a period of increased civilization. At about this time the very first Olympic Games were held. Only men were allowed to take part. Zeus married his sister Hera and he produced many more deities with her and in many other unions, the Graces, the Seasons and the Muses to mention a few. The relative peace did not last long, as the Giants taunted the Olympians by interfering in the running of the earth by diverting rivers, dislodging mountains and generally causing havoc until a great battle ensued: the Gigantomachy. Zeus reasserted his power as the king of the gods and restored the order of the universe. Zeus would be challenged yet again by the most feared god of all, the horrendous monster, Typhon, as tall as the stars and able to clasp the entire world in his hands. He had 100 dragons erupting from his neck with eyes that flashed fire and he was covered in wings. He was the product of the final mating of Gaia and Tartarus, and was determined to take over Mount Olympus. Zeus finally cornered him by using 100 lightning bolts at once and he placed Mount Etna over him to keep him in check. To this day mankind is threatened by Typhon, as the great beast tries to break free from his prison.

"How the gods must have chuckled when they added Hope to the evils
with which they filled Pandora's box, for they knew very well
that this was the cruelest evil of them all, since it is Hope that lures mankind to endure its misery to the end."

—W. Somerset Maugham; British author 1874–1965

Chapter Four

What Of Man? What Of Woman?

It may have struck you that all the gods had taken human form. This is one of the anomalies in Greek mythology; mortal man seems to have been very much an afterthought. They may have been created because the gods became tired of looking after themselves in terms of sustenance - they were perhaps created simply for the purposes of growing the crops that provided food, wine and fuel for fire for the gods. Some scholars suggest they were created simply as a diversion and amusement for the gods. They may have just provided extra fighting bodies for the gods in their endless battles. When Zeus appointed Prometheus and his brother Epimetheus to create men, his only stipulation had been that they should not have immortality.

It is interesting that Prometheus means "someone who evaluates before he acts" and Epimetheus means "someone who acts spontaneously and then evaluates." Prometheus tasked Epimetheus with creating many more creatures to inhabit the earth and equipping them with the various qualities and skills they needed to thrive and protect themselves: swiftness, strength, wings, claws, shells, cunning, fur etc. Prometheus in the meantime painstakingly fashioned man in clay and in the likeness of the gods. When he was finished, Epimetheus had used up all the special qualities and had nothing particular with which to endow man. Prometheus had acquired a fondness for the creature he was creating and decided the best he could do was to allow men to walk upright so that they could raise their eyes to heaven to praise the gods. He gave man the gift of fire as well. He then asked Athena to breathe life into man; this is how men came into existence. Zeus however was very displeased that man had acquired the gift of fire. In a fury he condemned Prometheus to be chained to a mountain for eternity. Every day a ferocious eagle would come to tear out and eat his liver. Because Prometheus he was immortal, his liver would regrow every night, dooming him go through the ordeal over and over. He was eventually rescued by the demigod Heracles.

Not content with Prometheus' punishment, and wanting to punish man as well, Zeus commanded Hephaestus to craft a woman so beautiful that she would "plague the hearts of men" forever. Although Hephaestus was the blacksmith of the gods, he was also a skilled craftsman and often produced decorative work of great beauty for the goddesses. The enchanting mortal, a female creature he fashioned from clay like man, was named Pandora, which means "the one who bears all gifts." Zeus commanded all the gods to each give her a gift which sounds very gracious until you hear that he instructed Hermes to teach her to be "deceitful, stubborn and curious."

Eventually the container, which might have been a box or more likely a storage jar, was filled with all the evils and miseries they could think of, including the plague and other contagious diseases, famine, poverty etc. It is clear that Zeus intended her as a punishment to mankind. She was instructed never to open the box under any circumstances and sent as a gift to wed Epimetheus. Initially Pandora obeyed the god's injunction, but eventually her curiosity got the better of her and she opened the box. She was overwhelmed by the horrible creatures that immediately escaped and spread around the entire world, bringing great harm. In a panic she slammed the lid down and, in one of the unfathomable ironies of the universe, the last creature, "Hope", was trapped inside the box.

Both Ovid and Hesiod talk about the ages of man. Ovid lists four ages and Hesiod, five. Neither list slips seamlessly into the generalized chronology of the creation of the universe. One must remember that all the sources of this ancient history were committed to writing hundreds of years after it was supposed to have taken place and by different writers, with different agendas at different times, so it is all a bit like the exegesis of the Christian scriptures. According to Hesiod the first age of man is known as their Golden Age and was a time when everyone lived in harmony and happiness. The animals could converse using human language. It was a time of abundance and even if death came, it came gently and at night when one was asleep. This was during the reign of Cronus. Then Cronus ate his children, which eventually caused the Titanomachy, and ten years of war brought this age to an end.

The gods then created the Silver Age of man. These mortals took a long time to grow up and never really matured. They remained very childish and disobedient, and would never pay proper heed to honoring the gods. Zeus became very impatient with their foolishness and destroyed them, sending their spirits to live in Hades.

Zeus soon grew bored without having mankind to toy with, so he created a brazen race of strong and warlike mortals. They were obsessed with weapons which they made of bronze; they built their homes of bronze as well - hence the Bronze Age of man. However they became consumed with their own aggression to such an extent that they ate no bread and destroyed each other, eating their victims' hearts instead. Zeus was so appalled at this cannibalism that he sent the Great Flood, or Deluge, to destroy them. Their spirits were banished to the Underworld. As a matter of interest, the year of the Flood in Christian orthodoxy is often set at c2348 BCE. In Greek mythography the date of the Great Flood or Deluge is usually calculated at c1456 BCE.

In the Age of Heroes that followed, Zeus seems to have got it right - just in time for the Trojan Wars and the war against Thebes. These mortals were however very noble and well respected by the gods, some so much so that they became demigods. Most were killed during the wars; however their spirits went to the Elysian Fields, were they received their rewards and lived in peace and happiness.

Finally Zeus created the Iron Age man – the age that persists today. Hesiod did not have anything good to say of this time: *"There will be no favour for the man who keeps his oath or for the just or for the good; but rather men will praise the evil-doer and his violent dealing. Strength will be right and reverence will cease to be; and the wicked will hurt the worthy man, speaking false words against him, and will swear an oath upon them.*" It is a gloomy outlook and a time of stress and failing morality. Men deceive each other and lie and no longer feel any shame in doing so. We age quickly and increasingly, evil will triumph and our gods will desert us – until Zeus comes again as the destroyer. Most of this information comes from Hesiod's *"Works and Days"* translated by Hugh G. Evelyn-White.

[*Hesiod. The Theogony of Hesiod and Works & Days.* Hugh G. Evelyn-White, trs. Create Space Independent Publishing Platform, 2011. Paperback ISBN-13:978-1460936450]

There is another version of the ending of the Bronze Age called the Deucalion myth. Deucalion was one of Prometheus' sons. In this version, Lycaon, King of Pelasgia, sacrificed a child to Zeus, angering the god greatly. Zeus turned the king into a wolf and decided to destroy the impious human race in a great flood. Prometheus warned his son and told him and his wife to build some kind of large chest that could survive the flood. This chest was large enough to hold them and some vital provisions, which enabled them to survive the deluge. After nine days and nights the flood waters started to recede and their boat came to rest on Mount Othrys in Thessaly (or Mount Parnassus in some versions). Deucalion and his wife Pyrrha wept when they saw the desolation and consulted the oracle Themis, asking how they might create a new and hopefully better race of humans. According to Ovid in his *Metamorphoses*, the answer they received was: *"With veiled heads and loosened robes throw behind you as you go the bones of your great mother."*

They were perplexed with the answer. Pyrrha was distraught at the idea of disturbing her mother's bones and wondered why they had been given advice which would certainly displease the gods. After some thought, they both took up stones, representing the "bones" from the earth, (their "great mother",) and cast them behind themselves as they walked. The hard stones started to soften and change shape and take on life: Deucalion's stones became men and Pyrrha's stones became women, thus restoring mankind.

Zeus was not displeased, as he regarded this couple as pious, observant and passionate about mankind. Earth herself regenerated all the other life forms, including the animals, as a result of the restorative rays of the sun meeting the moisture of the drying land. These were the people of the Age of Heroes, if you follow Hesiod's five ages, or, if you follow Ovid, who only records four ages, it was the start of the Age of Iron, the present age. It certainly accounts for man's hard-headedness and determination to survive.

"Is that which is holy loved by the gods because it is holy,
or is it holy because it is loved by the gods?"

Inscribed on the Temple of Apollo in Delphi.

Chapter Five

The Greek Pantheon

There are many other gods that go to make up the full pantheon of Greek mythology and support the intricate structure of the way the Greeks understood their world, but as far as the creation goes, in summary:

· Khaos produced Gaia

· Gaia birthed Uranus, Nyx, Pontus, Erebus and perhaps Aphrodite

· Gaia and Uranus mate and produce many children, the most important being the Titans

· Uranus is unseated by his Titan son, Cronus, who cuts off his father's genitals

· The blood of the genitals falls onto the earth, fertilizing Gaia, who produces more children, among whom are the Giants

· Semen from the genitals falls into the sea, probably creating Aphrodite

· Cronus becomes king, and marries his sister, Rhea

· Cronus is unseated by his son, Zeus, who becomes the god of the Olympians

· Rivalry with the Titans leads to the Titanomachy

· Zeus is victorious and commands the creation of man

· Zeus marries his sister, Hera

· Peace is destroyed by rivalry with the Giants which leads to the Gigantomachy

· Zeus is victorious again and the Olympians rule forever.

The bare bones of it are epic, violent, and driven by power struggles and sexual exploits.

The most important Olympians are: Zeus, Hera, Poseidon, Demeter, Athena, Apollo, Artemis, Ares, Aphrodite, Hephaestus, Hermes, Hestia and Dionysus.

Poseidon's parents were actually Titans and he is often shown with a dolphin, one of his sacred animals, or holding a trident. He is the god of the seas, rivers and horses and is sometimes mistaken for Zeus.

Hera was the Queen of the gods, Zeus' wife and sister. The marriage was tempestuous to say the least. She was extremely jealous and vengeful; this was not surprising, as Zeus was more unfaithful than most husbands. She was the goddess of women, marriage and childbirth. Her sacred animals were the cow and the peacock, and she is often depicted with a crown, a lotus staff or a lion.

Apollo is the only god whose name remains the same in Roman mythology. He was a complex god and very handsome, even beautiful, but always unlucky in love. He was much loved by the gods and was the god of music, prophecy, disease and healing, the sun and education. He is often depicted with a golden lyre or a silver bow and arrows. His most famous romance was when he fell in love with King Priam's daughter, Cassandra. In an effort to win her, he bestowed on her the gift of prophecy. When she finally spurned him, he kissed her goodbye and took away her powers of persuasion. Thereafter, although her prophecies always came true, no one ever believed her.

Artemis, the virgin goddess of the hunt and hunting, was Apollo's twin sister. She was also the goddess of chastity, choirs and the protector of children and wild animals. She is often shown with a bow and arrows, a spear, a lyre or accompanied by a deer. Her particular sacred animals are the deer, bear, wild boar, guinea fowl and quail. She was an intrepid hunter.

Demeter was the goddess of agriculture, grain and bread and the harvest. She taught man how to grow and utilize corn. Her sacred animals are serpents, swine and geckos and she is often shown with a sheaf of corn or a cornucopia. She had several lovers and children but her favorite was her daughter by Zeus, Persephone. Persephone was abducted by Hades and taken in secret to his domain, the Underworld. Demeter was distraught and neglecting all her duties, she searched desperately for her daughter. The crops stopped growing and started to wither and die. And soon the threat of famine hung over the earth. Zeus eventually intervened and struck a deal with Hades that Persephone could return to her mother. As she left, Hades gave Persephone a pomegranate to eat; this induced a spell which compelled her to return to Hades, for three months every year to visit him. This brings our winter, as Demeter once again grieves the loss of her special child.

Hymn to Athena
"I begin to sing of Pallas Athena,
the glorious goddess, bright-eyed, inventive, unbending
of heart,
pure virgin, saviour of cities, courageous, Tritogeneia.
From his awful head wise Zeus himself bare her
arrayed in warlike arms of flashing gold,
and awe seized all the gods as they gazed."

—Homer

Athene or Athena is the goddess of war, heroism, good council and olives. Her parents were Zeus and his first wife, Metis. Her birth was extraordinary: an oracle pronounced that Zeus' first child would be a girl and his second, a son, who would overthrow him, just as Zeus had overthrown his own father. When Metis was pregnant with her first child, Zeus devoured her, hoping to confound the prophecy. After a while he developed an intensely painful headache which caused him to scream out in agony. The other gods gathered about him and Hermes instructed Hephaestus to split open Zeus' skull whereupon Athene sprang out, fully clothed and prodigiously armed. According to Hesiod, Metis had more brains that all the men put together and this fact, and the manner in which her daughter was born, destined Athene to have an abundance of wisdom and intelligence. She remained a virgin and is usually depicted with a spear, helmet, and an *aegis,* a round shield decorated with a picture of Gorgon Medusa and rimmed with images of snakes. Athena was inventive and is credited with producing the first olive tree and several other useful inventions, like a bridle for handling horses. A colossal statue of her, crafted in gold and ivory, stood on the Acropolis in Athens until the 5th century CE when it was removed to Constantinople by the Byzantines -and disappeared somewhere along the way. What a heist that must have been!

Hermes is one of the busiest and most charming of all the gods. The god of travel, trade, thieves, animal husbandry, good luck, and language, he was also a guide to the dead and the herald of the gods. He was a bit of a prankster, but above everything else he was helpful - and there are as many stories of him getting up to mischief as there are of him helping people out of trouble. His father was Zeus and his mother a mountain nymph. He didn't marry, but legend has it that Pan is his son. He once stole Apollo's herd of sacred cattle and reversed their hooves so that the pursuers went in the opposite direction. He invented the lyre, playing dice and the alphabet. He is usually pictured with a winged hat and sandals, carrying a herald's staff.

Ares was a war god, much in the way that Athena was. However, he represented reality of war that required physical aggression and overwhelming force in lieu of Athene's intellectual strategizing. He was the child of Zeus and Hera and was also the god of battle and manliness. His sacred animal was the vulture and sometimes the dog. He was depicted with a helmet, a shield and a spear. He was Aphrodite's lover and in some versions of his story his daughters were the Amazons.

Hestia was the goddess of home, the family, the hearth, meals and sacrificial offerings, as well as architecture. She was the gentlest and mildest of the Olympians, a dedicated virgin and usually shown with a head veil, s branch of the Chaste tree and a kettle. Despite her retiring demeanor, every single meal in a Greek home began and ended with an offering made to her; in many city-states, a hearth in the local temple would be kept always burning for her. She had power of a different kind.

Hephaestus was the only god who was considered ugly and s disabled. In some versions of his creation he was born with a limp, in others he acquired the limp when one of his parents threw him off Olympia Mountain because he was imperfect. His mother was Hera, who is said to have birthed him on her own without Zeus. He became one of the key gods despite all this and was the god of metalwork, blacksmiths, fire, building, sculpture and volcanoes. He fashioned most of the gods' armaments, including the shields belonging to Zeus and Athene. He was very gentle and a patron of the arts. His sacred animals were the donkey and the crane, and he is often depicted as riding a donkey and with an anvil, hammer and tongs to hand. His marriage to Aphrodite was arranged by Zeus; the issue of that union, Ericthonius, was half man and half serpent.

These 12 gods were known as the Olympians and they ruled over all the other gods, the universe and every aspect of human existence. Dionysus, a special case, can be found later.

Achilles speaking to the seer Calchas.
Prophet of evil, when have you ever said
good things to me? You love to foretell the worst,
always the worst! You never show good news.
—Homer; Iliad. Book I

Chapter Six

The Trojan War

The Trojan War is one of the greatest stories of all time. In the 12th and 13th centuries it was regarded as historical fact and consisted of the Greek army, led by Agamemnon, crossing the seas to Sparta in over a thousand ships to demand, or fight for, the return of Menelaus' wife, Helen, who had absconded with Prince Paris. By the mid-19th century it had been relegated to a mythological event. In 1870 an archaeologist named Heinrich Schliemann startled the world by unearthing the ancient city of Troy, the incontestable relics of an ancient, long-running conflict and the remnants of King Priam's treasures at Hisarlik in Turkey. By then, the writings of Eratosthenes, the librarian of the Great Library of Alexandria, had been studied. He had written a Chronography of dates of important events, noting the Trojan War from 1194–1184 BCE. The Schliemann site actually contained many cities built one upon another, and Wilhelm Dörpfeld, who had been Schliemann's young assistant, confirmed level Vll-*a* of the excavations as Homeric Troy in 1893.

If you read the *Iliad* by Homer you will learn a great deal of Greek mythology, especially if you read the back-stories of the heroes involved. The *Iliad* itself only covers 53 days at the end of the 10th year of the war, but the ramifications of the event stretch over 20 years at least.

It all began with a golden apple inscribed with the words: *"For the fairest"*. This was a wedding gift, hurled to the floor by Eris, the goddess of Discord, when she discovered that she alone among the gods had not been invited to the wedding of the goddess Thetis, to a worthy mortal, Peleus. Hera, Athene and Aphrodite laid claim to the apple and the Trojan Prince, Paris, was appointed to arbitrate. Athene offered Paris wisdom and the skill of a great warrior if he chose her as the winner; Hera offered him political power and control of the whole of Asia as an inducement; Aphrodite offered him the hand of the most beautiful woman in the world, Helen of Sparta, should he chose her. Paris chose Aphrodite and set off to Sparta, on a "diplomatic mission" to claim his prize, Helen, who just happened to be married to the King of Sparta, Menelaus. As the 20 year epic tale unfolds there are more ramifications than a television soap opera; there are as many betrayals, cliff-hangers, tissue box moments, impossible choices, disastrous decisions and monumental dilemmas as one can imagine, all interspersed with constant interference from the gods (literal moments of "deus ex machina"), to facilitate the developments and outcomes they desire.

Let me illustrate with a few examples.

Aphrodite causes Helen to fall in love with Paris as soon she sets eyes on him. When Menelaus had to attend a state funeral far from home, Paris woos and abducts her and sets off for his home in Troy. There has been much debate over whether Helen went willingly or not and whether she took state assets with her or not.

The seer Calchas made several prophecies about the Trojan war; one of the first being that Troy would only fall if the expedition included the two great warriors Achilles and Odysseus. This caused a delay especially as Odysseus, a shrewd, eloquent and skilled if atypical hero, did not actually want to go. He pretended to be deranged to avoid being conscripted. He was sowing his fields with salt instead of seed as part of faking this madness when the messenger arrived. Unfortunately the conscripting officer placed Odysseus' young son in the path of the plough and when Odysseus took avoiding action, his ruse was revealed. Odysseus reluctantly left his home, knowing it would be twenty years before he returned. Achilles was fifteen years old when he left for the war, with his father's body armor that had been fashioned for him by Hephaestus. He would not return.

A second dreadful pronouncement was that Agamemnon, who led the expedition, had offended the goddess Artemis, and he would have to sacrifice his daughter Iphigenia to her before the becalmed winds would blow allowing the fleet to sail. As the agonized father raised his dagger to deal the fatal stroke a heavy fog descended on the altar. When it cleared Iphigenia's little body had been replaced by a fawn, presumably by Artemis. Hesiod says that Iphigenia became the goddess Hecate.

When the Greeks eventually encamped outside the impenetrable walls of Troy, Paris refused to return Helen and the siege began. This became a way of life for the participants. At one stage, in an effort to break the impasse a duel was arranged between Menelaus and Paris.

"*At once, they ceased their attack and fell silent, while Hector spoke to both the armies: 'Listen, you Trojans, and you bronze-greaved Greeks, these are the words of Paris, source of all this strife. He asks that both sides ground their sharp weapons while he and Menelaus, beloved of Ares, fight in single combat between the armies, for Helen and all her treasure. Whichever wins and shows himself the better man let him take both wealth and woman to his house, while the rest of us sign a treaty under oath.'*
When he finished, silence reigned, till Menelaus of the loud war-cry spoke: 'Hear me, now. Mine is the heart that suffered most: I propose that Greeks and Trojans part in peace, for you have borne much pain through this quarrel of mine with Paris, though he began it. Whichever of us is fated to die: let him fall; the rest of you shall leave swiftly in peace. Bring two sheep, white ram and black ewe, to sacrifice to Earth and Sun, and we will bring another for Zeus, and let great Priam swear the oath himself ....'
The Greeks and Trojans thrilled to his words, seeing an end to the pain of war. The chariots were reined in along the lines, and the charioteers descended, and shed their battle gear in tightly-spaced piles on the ground. Meanwhile Hector sent two runners to the city to summon Priam and bring the sacrifice. Likewise King Agamemnon sent [one] to the hollow ships, telling him to return with a lamb. He straight obeyed."
—Homer; Iliad. Book III

A great duel took place between the two. Towards the end, when both had lost their weapons, Menelaus "threw himself on Paris, seizing him by his helm's thick horsehair crest, whirled him round and dragged him towards the Achaean lines. Paris was choked by the richly inlaid strap of his helm, drawn tight beneath his chin, pressing on his soft throat. And Menelaus would have hauled him off and won endless glory, had not Zeus' daughter Aphrodite, swift to see it, broken the ox-hide strap, so the empty helm was left in Menelaus' strong grip." [Homer; Iliad. Book III]

The gods even had a hand in the terrible death of the darling of the Trojan War, Achilles. During one of the many attempts on the walls of Troy an arrow from Paris, **guided by Apollo,** pierces Achilles' heel, leading to his death.

Odysseus is the one that finally engineers the end of the war with the deception of the Trojan Horse. Pretending to give up and return home, the Greeks leave "a gift" of a colossal wooden horse for their enemies and retreat out of sight. The horse is drawn into the city and Troy celebrates the end of the siege. In the early hours of the morning, the handpicked warriors hiding inside the horse open the impenetrable gates and Agamemnon finally leads the Greek army into the city and victory. At many points in the story, especially when a god intervenes, the sources record that "it is not yet time" for the event concerned to occur – the timekeeper was perhaps the great Olympian god Zeus, watching with amusement the happenings below.

Electra receives the urn containing her brother's ashes.

"But now, an exile from home and fatherland, thou
hast perished miserably,
far from thy sister; woe is me, these loving hands have
not washed or
decked thy corpse, nor taken up, as was meet, their sad
burden from the flaming pyre.
No! at the hands of strangers, hapless one, thou hast
had those rites,
and so art come to us, a little dust in a narrow urn...

Ah me, ah me! O piteous dust! Alas, thou dear one, sent on
a dire journey,

how hast undone me,- undone me indeed,
O brother mine!"
— Sophocles; Electra.

Chapter Seven

The Influence Of Greek Drama

A major contributing factor affecting how much has come down to us about Greek mythology is the tradition of public discourse, oratory and dramatic presentation in classical Greece. This flourished around the god Dionysus and the many festivals honoring him. Dionysus was the only god who had a mortal mother and said to have been "twice-born". Zeus' lascivious eye fell upon a Theban princess called Semele, and he took to visiting her undercover as a "divine presence" rather than as a man. Once she realized she was pregnant by him, she made Zeus promise to grant her one wish, which he did. She asked to see him as he was in his immortal form and she died in a great burst of flaming glory as he revealed himself in all his power and majesty. Zeus retrieved the fetal child and stitched him into his thigh to carry him to term. Zeus' wife, Hera, in a fit of jealous rage, dispatched a few Titans to rip the child to pieces. However the goddess Rhea brought him back to life and presented him to Zeus. Zeus became particularly enchanted with this child and sent him to be raised in safety by the nymphs of Mount Nysa. *Dios* means "of Zeus" and so he was named Dionysus.

Dionysus is credited with inventing the art of viticulture. He was the god of fertility, wine, ritual madness, pleasure, festivity, parties and the theatre. His sacred animals are the leopard, lynx and tiger and very specifically, the sexually potent goat; especially the satyrs, who were half man and half goat. He travelled widely and was generally regarded as the "bad boy" of Olympus. Once he was abducted by pirates who didn't realize his powers. He changed the ship's mast into a massive vine and the sails dripped with wine. He turned himself into a lion and with the help of a bear, *he dispatched the pirate captain. In terror, the remaining crew members leapt overboard and were changed into dolphins.* He spared the helmsman, as he had been the only one who had voted against Dionysus being "press-ganged", and they sailed on to Naxos.

Several festivals were held in his honor, all of which typically involved a great deal of eating, drinking and dancing in enormous street parties. Devotees dressed in goat skins pretended to be satyrs and behaved like them. There were parades of worshipers carrying phallic objects through the streets of Grecian city-states; the more devout would literally become deliriously drunk and indulge in sexual orgies and other debaucheries. The most important event by far though was held in Athens, from the 9th to the 13th of March, every year. It was called the City Dionysia, and took the form of a great literary competition for writers, particularly dramatists. The greatest writers of the day took part.

Aeschylus lived from 525–456 BCE and wrote tragedies that won many prizes at the Dionysia. We have 7 surviving texts: *Agamemnon; The Choephori; Eumenides; The Persians; Prometheus Bound; The Seven Against Thebes* and *The Suppliants.* He was also an actor and there was an attempt to assassinate him on stage as a result of initiation rituals he had revealed: the Eleusinian Mysteries, used in the cult of Demeter and Persephone. *"Agamemnon"* won first prize in 458 BCE and tells the story of his return to his wife Clytemnestra after the Trojan Wars. Clytemnestra kills him and Cassandra, the mistress he brings back with him, with her own hands, in revenge for his sacrifice of Iphigenia.

Sophocles (496–409 BCE) was also an actor, and he is remembered as the tragedian who extended the number of actors used in a play and was thus able to take the themes beyond a dialogue about religion and morality into an interactive dramatic performance. He wrote well over 100 plays of which seven complete texts survive: *Antigone; Electra; Oedipus at Colonus; Oedipus the King, Philoctetes and Trachinian Women.* He was 28 when he won first place at the Dionysia, dislodging Aeschylus. *"Electra"* was written quite late in his life and must be one of the most moving of the tragedies. Electra was Agamemnon's daughter and Iphigenia's sister. She had sent her beloved brother into hiding soon after Agamemnon departed for the Trojan Wars, when she suspected he might be in danger from her mother's lover, Aegisthus. The play *"Electra"* deals with the revenge she takes on her mother and Aegisthus when they kill Agamemnon on his return from Troy. The extract above occurs when she is told her brother has been killed and she receives his ashes and realizes that she alone must exact the revenge.

Euripedes was born in 480 BCE and was also a prolific poet and dramatist. He wrote about 90 plays, of which 17 survive. He first entered the City Dionysia in 455 BCE and won a first prize in 441 BCE, the first of four. He also based much of his work on popular myths of the time but he was more critical of the content than others, and he was known for developing complex female protagonists like Medea, Hecuba and Andromache. He also wrote a play on the Electra story. His most powerful texts were *Medea, Hippolytus, Alcestis and The Bacchae*. He died in Macedonia in 406 BCE. *"The Bacchae"* is about Dionysus, who returns to the city of his birth, Thebes, to vindicate his mother Semele and to claim acknowledgement as one of the gods. Essentially, it is a serious play about reason versus irrationality. *"It demonstrates the necessity of self-control, moderation and wisdom in avoiding the two extremes: both the tyranny of excessive order, and the murderous frenzy of collective passion."* [Luke Mastin 2009] Available at: http://www.ancient-literature.com/greece_euripides_bacchae.html. It won a fifth first prize at the City Dionysia for Euripides posthumously.

One of the requirements governing the Dionysia was that any writer who entered had to present at least one satirical play or a substantial comedy.

Aristophanes (c456–c380 BCE) is the best remembered gifted writer of comedies. He wrote 30 plays but only eleven texts have survived. He is best remembered for *"The Birds,"* in which he satirized the idea of democracy; *"The Clouds"*; a serious critical attack on Sophocles, and *"Lysistrata"* in which he mocked war. The latter is still often performed today and still carries a bite; in a bid to end the Peloponnesian Wars, Lysistrata convinces all the women to withhold sex from their men until a peace treaty is negotiated. The women also take over the treasury on the Akropolis in order to control the finances that facilitate the war.

Chapter Eight

Two Greek Mortal Heroes In Mythological Tales

Theseus and the Slaying of the Minotaur. In the *Iliad*, Nestor says that among all the heroes of the Trojan War, none was greater than Theseus. Theseus was a mortal famous for many deeds of valor, including killing the Centaur of Minos on Crete. The creature was half man and half bull and was born to Queen Pasiphae after Zeus had visited her in the form of a bull. There are many variations in this particular myth and in some versions the bull was actually a gift to Minos from the god Poseidon. King Minos of Crete felt he couldn't kill the creature, so he imprisoned him in an elaborate labyrinth he had designed by the famous architect Daedalus. This maze provided a convenient way of disposing of his enemies as well as feeding the centaur that only ate human flesh. Unfortunately when Minos' son Androgeus went to the games in Athens, he was killed by the same bull that had visited his mother. In his anger and grief, King Minos demanded an annual tribute from Athens in the form of 7 young men and 7 young women to be sacrificed to the Minotaur. The King of Athens, in fear of the dreaded might of Minos, complied for the first two years. In the third year his son Theseus commits himself to end this dreadful situation and, very much against his father King Aegeus' wishes, he volunteers himself as a sacrifice and sets sail. The King makes him promise that if he survives, he will set white sails on his return home. Theseus announces his intention of killing the Minotaur to King Minos and his daughter, Ariadne, realizes that even if Theseus succeeds in killing the dreaded beast, he will still perish trying to find his way out of the labyrinth. She gives him a ball of wool to unwind as he seeks the monster's den and to follow on the way back. She also asks him to take her with him when he goes home. Theseus is able to overcome the monster and find his way back to the entrance and he sets sail for home, taking Ariadne with him. They have a difficult voyage home, fighting really bad weather and tempestuous storms, requiring many of the sails to be repaired and replaced, using the spare set of black sails. King Aegeus, keeping watch from a high cliff outlook, sees the black sails on the horizon and, thinking his son is lost, casts himself into the raging sea below. Ever since that day that sea is called the Aegean in honor of his grief.

Jason and the Golden Fleece. Jason came to fame as a hero before the Trojan War. Pelias usurped the throne of Iolcus (present day Volos) by imprisoning his brother, Aeson, the rightful heir. He received a warning from an oracle that a descendent of Aeson would take revenge on him and he sends Jason, Aeson's son, on a quest to retrieve the Golden Fleece. The Golden Fleece was the skin of a ram sacred to Zeus that was kept in the Temple of Ares, the god of war, and guarded by an impressive dragon, in the land of Colchis. Aeson presumed that Jason would meet his death on the journey as this was regarded as an impossible mission. Jason was bright as well as intrepid and he gathered around him a band of 50 warriors including, in some versions of the story, great heroes like Heracles. A fine ship was built and named Argos after the designer, Argus, and after suitable blessings were sought the men set forth. This mission became known as the Argonautica. After an adventurous journey, charting the waters of the Black Sea for the first time, they arrived in Colchis and requested the prize from the ruler King Aeetes, in the name of the goddess Hera. Not wanting to give up the prize but hesitant to displease the gods, King Aeetes sets Jason a prohibitive trial: yoke two fire-breathing bulls with metallic legs, plough a large field and then sow the field with dragon's teeth. He neglected to tell him that this would result in an army of warriors rising from the earth that would tackle him and his paltry party. Fortunately, the King's daughter, Medea, was impressed with Jason and, being a bit of a sorceress and the granddaughter of the sun god Helios, (and really very bad news if only he had known!) she gave him a protective potion to make him impermeable to fire and iron for 24 hours. She also and told him about her father's plan and what to do about it. When the army rose from the ground Jason threw a large stone into their midst; thinking it was an attack, the men turned on each other and they fought to the death, eliminating each other completely. Aeetes had to give Jason permission to retrieve the Golden Fleece, hoping this time that the dragon would slay him. Medea stepped in again and put a spell on the dragon so that Jason was able to retrieve the sacred prize with ease. As Jason and the Argonauts boarded the Argo and prepared to depart, Medea abducted her brother and then joined them. As they sailed away, she killed her brother and cut him to pieces, spreading his body parts in the way of the perusing ship. This slowed Aeetes, as he tried to retrieve all the bits and pieces of his son. Many years later, in another great myth, Medea would kill her own children that she had with Jason. But this story belongs to the brave Jason and his Argonauts. After many further trials and tribulations he lays the precious Golden Fleece at the feet of King Pelias.

Conclusion

Greek mythology is complex, and although the creation of mortals seems to have been an afterthought and embarked upon mainly for the vast entertainment of the Olympians, as these myths developed, an intense interaction between gods, demi-gods and heroic and no- so heroic mortals manifests. The heritage of the great Classical Period from c480 to 323 BCE, which includes the famous philosophers and the great dramatic playwrights, is certainly germane to us all to this very day. By 336 BCE Greek language, literature, culture and religious beliefs were appreciated throughout the civilized world and certainly anywhere touched by Alexander the Great. In 192 BCE the Spartan monarchy collapsed and Sparta came under Roman rule; by 168 BCE, Perseus, the last king of Macedonia, also fell under the Roman yoke.

It is a mistake to think that the Romans simply took over Greek mythology, though most of the Greek gods do have a Roman counterpart. The Roman gods had a very different kind of persona and the syncretization of the two beliefs involved a complex and sometimes conflicted process. Still, in 145 BCE Greece became part of the Roman Empire. I wonder what Zeus had to say about that?

"Myths are public dreams, dreams are private myths."
—Joseph Campbell; American mythologist 1904-1987

NORSE MYTHOLOGY

A Concise Guide to Gods, Heroes, Sagas and Beliefs of Norse Mythology

Introduction

If this is indeed your first foray into the subject of Norse mythology, you will find that it calls for an adjustment in the way you see things. You will need to prepare yourself for a very different world, one where there is often no logic as you understand it, no justice as administered by a modern court of law, and very little point in asking "why." An amazing world where animals have the power of speech, inanimate objects like swords or hammers have specific names, and where the passage of time is measured by the destruction of the world. It is nevertheless a fascinating, illuminating and richly rewarding world, and your appreciation of where, how and why you exist will be immeasurably enhanced by what you discover.

Norse mythology covers the pre-Christian history of the countries and peoples of what we now call Scandinavia. The cosmology presents us with a theory of the creation of the world and the first people who dwelt here. These were the guiding beliefs of the people we call the Vikings, who were the adventurers who set off from modern Norway, Sweden and Denmark and swept through ancient Britain, a nascent Europe and on into Russia and India in medieval times. Initially appearing and behaving as pillaging raiders from the sea, they built trade routes through the world that are still used to this very day. Their strength and success lay in their skills as ship builders and seafarers and their unshakable pagan beliefs in predestination, which dictated that the only honourable way to die was in battle. These were the

Norsemen, and one of their descendents is the star of this story.

Snorre Sturleson (1179-1241) was orphaned at an early age and was brought up by Jón Loptsson, possibly the most influential Chieftain in Iceland. Snorre married money and settled in Reykjaholt, acquiring a reputation as a scholar, writer and historian. He was elected twice as the "lawspeaker" in the Iceland High Court. He collected together and wrote down as many of the old oral poems on gods and heroes as he could find. He also added his own commentary and extensive writings into what became a kind of poetic handbook which has come down to us as the Prose Edda, with "Edda" meaning "great grandmother." One of his sources, a collection of poems by Saemund Sigfusson, was found in 1643 in an old farmhouse in Oddi. This is now known as the Poetic or Elder Edda and it contains some tales from as early as 800 BCE, riddle contests between the gods and the giants, and an amazing version of the creation of the world. Incredibly, these two books are by far the most important and authentic source of Norse mythology that we have, and all as a result of the intense interest of one man! There are a few other sources available, but with all being transcriptions of oral history that was recorded hundreds of years after the event and, like the Snorre collection, usually by a Christian. One of the reasons that the Eddas are such a trustworthy source is that we know from contemporary sources that, although Snorre was Christian, he did not hold the popular opinion that pagan gods were manifestations or personifications of Satan.

The Eddas are freely available to be read online as a result of the Project Gutenberg and you can find them at: http://www.gutenberg.org/files/14726/14726-h/14726-h.htm Unless otherwise stated, all quotes used herein come from this specific source. The translations are done from Old Norse by Benjamin Thorpe and I.A. Blackwell. While Snorre sadly came to an untimely end as a result of falling out with the King of Norway, who ordered his assassination, his legacy lives on.

Another paradigm shift we must make before we enter the realm of ancient mythology is the place of the Gods in daily life, how real and present they were, and how important. Most people tend to know more about the mythological Greek and Roman pantheons than their Norse counterparts, as they were a much jollier lot. The Greek gods in particular lived a pleasurable and joyous life in Olympus - they were immortal, having been created by Mother Earth and Father Heaven. The great Greek heroes were modelled in their likeness and were beautiful, fearless and performed daring feats with strength and courage. The Norse gods were more remarkable, not immortal and constantly at odds with their Giant enemies. They endured great trials and lived in Asgard, which they knew was destined to go up in flames during Ragnarok, or the prophesized end of the world. The Greek gods came before and in fact, created the universe, while in Norse mythology, the universe was created by and from one of the gods. Norse heroes, though similarly enormously strong, were unlike their Greek and Roman counterparts; as they were strangely detached, almost solemn, and tended to be tested by performing feats that demanded great sacrifices. Interestingly, in both mythologies gods and goddesses had equal rights and were just as powerful and forthright.

Chapter One

The Creation in Norse Mythology

"Twas time's first dawn,

When nought yet was,

Nor sand nor sea,

Nor cooling wave;

Earth was not there,

Nor heaven above.

Nought save a void

And yawning gulf.

But verdure none."

The "void and yawning gulf" was called Ginnunngagap. To the north was a frozen waste of ice, fog, frost and bitter cold called Niflheim. In the south was a wasteland called Muspelheim, consumed with fire, smoke, sparks and oozing lava. These two spheres drifted towards each other through the void, finally colliding; if this sounds vaguely familiar, it is because it echoes the first verses of Genesis in the Bible: "The earth was without form and void, and darkness was over the face of the deep." But then, all familiarity disappears and in the Eddas we read: "And when the heated blast met the gelid vapour it melted it into drops, and, by the might of him who sent the heat, these drops quickened into life, and took a human semblance. The being thus formed was named Ymir." Ymir is variously described as "the primordial deity or Ice Giant" or a "humanoid creature". At the same time and from the same material, the cow Audhumbla was created. Four rivers of milk flowed from her teats which sustained Ymir, who fell asleep after drinking large quantities of her milk. As he slept, two giants, one male and one female, grew from the sweat under Ymir's left armpit. Some versions of the myth say that one giant came from each armpit. Even more startlingly, his legs parted, creating a son called Thrudgelmir or "Strength Yeller." In one version it was actually a six-headed son that grew out of his feet. However it happened, this was the first of the Frost Giants or the Jotuns.

Audhumbla, the giant cow, sustained herself by licking the salt from the rocks. On the first day, her licking produced an outline of long hair; the second produced a human head and the third revealed the rest of the body of Buri, the first God. Buri immediately produced a son called Bor or Borr. Borr married a Jotun named Bestla and they had three mighty sons: Odin, Vile and Vé.

The Creation of the Earth

It was then, even before the forming of the Earth, that the eternal feud between good and evil began. The Prose Edda records it thus:

"Was there," asked Gangler, "any kind of equality or any degree of good understanding between these two races?"
"Far from it," replied Har; "for the sons of Bor slew the giant Ymir, and when he fell there ran so much blood from his wounds, that the whole race of Frost-giants was drowned in it, except a single giant, who saved himself with his household." It is not clear why Ymir was killed and if one visualizes a race of giants drowning in the subsequent bloodshed. One is bound to want to know the reason for such overwhelming brutality, but as I mentioned above, the one thing we must not do on this journey is ask "why."

The earth was then created by Bor, Odin, Vile and Vé out of Ymir's body. From his flesh they fashioned the Earth. Using his eyebrows and jaws they built an island stronghold to protect themselves from the Giants and called it Midgard; out of his blood, the seas and lakes were created; out of his bones, the mountains and hills; out of his hair the trees and grasses were fashioned. His skull became the heavens and his brains were scattered to form the clouds. Worms or maggots crawled out of his skull and these became the race of dwarves. Four dwarves were chosen to hold up the four corners of the sky: Nordi held up the North; Sundri, the South; Austri the East and Vestri, the West. The stars were fashioned from the sparks and burning embers that remained from the tremendous conflagration in Ginnunngagap.

The Axis of the Universe

"There stands an ash called Yggdrasil,

A mighty tree showered in white hail.

From there come the dews that fall in the valleys.

It stands evergreen above Urd's Well."

One of the central structures in Norse mythology is the evergreen ash tree called Yggdrasil. There are conflicting versions of how it came to be but it is regarded as the holiest seat of the Gods and where they hold council every day. Some say that, like the Earth, it came from Ymir's body and some say it is one with Odin. The nine worlds (see next section) are supported in its branches or enclosed in its three great roots. It draws water from the sacred Well of Urd. This well is pivotal in Norse mythology and we will return to it time and time again. The waters are so sacred that they run white as an eggshell. This is perhaps this is the first time that the colour white, which encompasses the entire colour spectrum, is associated with purity, new beginnings and awakenings. Two pure white swans – the progenitors of the entire race, are born from this well. Perched at the top of the tree is an omniscient eagle whose flapping wings provide the great winds that encircle the Earth. Between his eyes sits an eagle called Vedurfolnir. At the bottom of the tree lives Nidhog, a dragon, who gnaws at its roots. The eagle and Nidhog detest each other and spend a great deal of time trading insults via Ratatosk, a gossipy squirrel who runs between the two as a messenger all day. Four stags also live in the branches: Dáinn; Dvallin; Duneyrr and Duraprór. A great many serpents keep company with Nidhog. This cosmic tree is maintained by three women who appear in similar guises in Greek, Roman and Norse mythology and are very important to both Gods and humans; the Fates who determine our destiny. In the Greek and Roman pantheon they represent the "thread of life," the "length of the thread," and the "cutter of the thread." In Norse mythology they are Urder, she who knows the past, Verdandi, she who controls the present, and Skuld, the youngest, who prepares the future. They water the roots of the tree every day from the Well of Urd and, each morning, they put a very noisy rooster at the top of the tree. They don't tolerate much back-chat either.

The Creation of Humans

One day, Bor's sons were strolling along the beach and they found two logs – one from an ash tree and one from an elm tree. From each log they fashioned a human being; one male and one female. Odin gave them life and a lively spirit; Vili gifted them shape, speech, feelings and five senses, and Vé endowed them with movement, mind and intelligence. The man was named Ask and the woman was named Embla. "From these two descend the whole human race whose assigned dwelling was within Midgard."

A man called Mundilfari quickly caused the Gods some chagrin. He had two children who were breathtakingly lovely to look on. He named his gentle and graceful daughter Sol (sun) and the striking and handsome son, Mani (moon). The Gods, finding this very presumptuous, placed the children in the heavens and Sol was commanded to drive the horses, Arvak (Early Rising) and Alsvid (Very Fast), who pulled the chariot of the sun the gods had made to give light to the earth, across the sky. Her brother Mani was told to guide the passage of the moon and control its waxing and waning.

Odin, also known as the All-father, used the same kind of strategy to form the night and the day - but this time he turned to the Jotuns instead: "Then took All-father, [Nott] Night, and [Dagr] Day, her son, and gave them two horses and two cars, and set them up in the heavens that they might drive successively one after the other, each in twelve hours' time, round the world." The first to ride out is Night, on her horse who is called Hrimfaxi. The night ride is long and, as he comes to the end of the journey, his coat is gleaming and covered in foam. As he shakes his bridle the foam covers the earth and humans see it as light dew as the day breaks. Skinfaxi is the name of Day's horse; his mane is so luxurious and full that it sheds light over heaven and earth.

Chapter Two

The Nine Worlds of Norse Mythology

Three of these worlds are above the Earth. The first of these is the headquarters of the Æsir Gods, Asgard; sometimes referred to as Asgarör. It has 540 halls. One of these is the hall that belongs to Odin. It is called Valaskjalf and it stands out even among the other great dwellings because of its pure silver roof. Some sources say that the entire building was made of silver. The throne is called Hlidskjalf and when Odin sits in it, he can see over the entire world. On the far side is a rainbow bridge which allows the Gods passage to the world of men. This bridge is called Bifrost. "The gods made a bridge from earth to heaven, and called it Bifrost. Thou must surely have seen it; but, perhaps, thou callest it the rainbow." Dead heroes will pass through Asgard on their way to dwell in Valhalla. Thrudheim, the Place of Might, is also located here and this is where you will find Thor when he is not busy.

Muspelheim, or Muspell, is the second of these worlds considered to be "above" the Earth. This is the land of primordial fire, ruled by the evil fire giant Surt ("Black") who guards the entrance with a blazing sword. Surt has burning hair and is covered in glowing lava, and has little to do in Norse mythology until the end of the world, when he plays a pivotal role. Essentially, Muspelheim is a no-man's land, though some sources say that the fire giants and fire demons dwell here. "Muspell is a world too luminous and glowing to be entered by those who are not indigenous there."

The third world set above the earth is **Alfheimr**, the home of the Light Elves. These are the beautiful and youthful minor gods of nature and fertility. Considered to bring inspiration in the spheres of art and music and ruled by the major god Freyr. Sometimes mocked and described as "puny" because of their lightness and luminosity, they can easily punch above their weight as they are highly skilled in the art of magic.

The main world located on the Earth is **Midgard**, sometimes called Mannheim, or the world of humans. The entire world is encircled by an evil serpent, Jormungand, who stabilises his hold by biting his own tail. Bifrost ends in Midgard.

The second Earth-bound world is Vanaheim, or **Vanaheimr** and it is also the home of the Vanir, gods but a particular group of gods separate from the Æsir! These Vanir are particularly associated with fertility, wisdom and the ability to see into the future. The trouble between the gods started when the Vanir goddess Freya visited Asgard. Freya practiced a powerful kind of witchcraft which could manipulate one's destiny. The Æsir found this very seductive and often used her services. Eventually, they began to realize that they were being led astray from their basic beliefs by their own greedy desires. However instead of looking at themselves for the fault, they turned on her Freya instead, calling her her Gullveig, or "greedy for gold." The Æesir attempted to kill Freya, but she rose from her own ashes three times. Unwisely, the Æesir decided to go to war with the Vanir, even after such a display of immortality. "Broken was the outer wall of the Æsir's burgh. The Vanir, foreseeing conflict, tramp o'er the plains. Odin cast [his spear], and mid the people hurled it: that was the first warfare in the world."

Neither side could gain the upper hand for long and fairly soon the divinities became weary and bored by the fighting. As such, a truce was declared. To establish and cement good faith, each side sent several "hostages" to live with the other tribe. Freya, Freyr and Njord went to live in Asgard and Hoenir and Mimer moved to Vanaheim. This truce has been honoured and, although their spheres of expertise are different, they often overlap with no friction and both "tribes" or "races" have important roles to play. For instance, the guardian of the vital Bifrost bridge is the Vanir god, Heimdall.

The last earth-bound world is that of **Jutunheim**. This is the realm of the Jotuns or Giants, also known as Etins. It is a cold place and flat around the edges, rocky and mountainous with overgrown, wild forests towards the interior. There are Frost or Rime Giants; Ice Giants; Mountain Giants and Storm Giants. They are between twenty to thirty feet tall; strong with flesh and bone density three times that of humans. They are vulnerable to heat and function best in their own environment. The Giant god Mimir's Well of Wisdom is placed here, where he guards it. Often referred to as the god of prophecy, Mimir remained so still that he became part of a great mountain surrounding the well. The Jutun are constantly at loggerheads with the Æsir. They are led by Utgard-Loki, the Æsir god of mischief; despite implacable dislike between the Frost Giants and the Æsir, there is much intermarriage between two. Loki himself is the son of the Giant king Lunvey. Additionally, the Jotun were technically there first: the very first deity that was created was Ymir, after all.

This brings us to the three underground worlds said to be among the roots of the Cosmic Tree – things get a bit murky here, as not all sources agree with one another. Firstly there is **Svartalfheim**, the world of the Dark Elves. These creatures hate the light and the sun and will turn to stone if exposed to either. They annoy and threaten humans a great deal mainly via nightmares or by haunting animals. This may also be where the dwarves reside as well – it is not clear.

Next is **Nidavellir**. This is where most sources put the realm of the dwarves. The dwarves play a vital part in Norse Mythology mainly because they are such excellent craftsmen. In addition to being the most gifted at craftwork they are also masters of magic and sorcery. They are constantly being called upon by the gods to create important, ingenious and clever artifacts for all kinds of occasions, typically being requested to craft crowns, jewellery, fetters, magic containers, weapons, vases, and so on. Many of the myths actually depend on the result of their skills, such as when Odin was at his wits end on how to bind the ferocious wolf Fenrir. Odin sent a messenger into Nidavellir looking for a craftsman skilled enough to finally create something that would restrain Fenrir. It was obvious that whatever it was needed to be backed up by some kind of sorcery to render it fail-safe, but dwarves were up for the challenge. They forged a restraint called Gleipnir. "It was fashioned out of six things; to wit, the noise made by the footfall of a cat; the beards of women; the roots of stones; the sinews of bears; the breath of fish; and the spittle of birds." When applied, it was the first restraint to work! This quote from the Eddas demonstrates the confusion as to where the dwarves actually reside.

Finally, there is **Niflheim**; the place of the mists and the coldest and most inhospitable world. Here is located the well of Hvergelmir which means "bubbling" or "boiling spring". Hvergelmir is guarded by the dragon Nidhug and it is the point from which all living proceeded and to which all living will return. The Eddas say that there is a gate in this world that opens into "the abode of death." This refers to the fact that, deep inside Niflheim is Helheim, the realm of the dead. It is ruled by the Goddess Hel or Hela and it is the home of those who do not die in battle. Unlike the Christian Hell, it is as icy and cold.

Chapter Three

The Major Gods and Goddesses

When one is exploring the world of the gods and goddesses, it is as well to remember that several of them go by different names at different times. They are also very good at assuming names for short periods, particularly when they are on a "mission" of some sort, more often than not because they are up to some sort of mischief! When, for instance, Freya visited Asgard, precipitating the Æsir/Vanir war, she went in disguise as Heiðr or "Bright", a sorcerer. An excellent online source of brief biographies for the many gods and goddesses you will come across at: http://www.sunnyway.com/runes/gods2.html , but here are some of the most important characters.

Odin is the main and key god in Norse mythology. Not to put too fine a point on it, he said: "I call myself Grim and Ganglari, Herian, Hialmberi, Thekk, Third, Thunn, Unn, Helblindi, High, Sann, Svipal, Sanngetal, Herteit, Hnikar, Bileyg, Baleyg, Bolverk, Fiolnir, Grimnir, Glapsvinn, Fiolsvinn, Sidhott, Sidskegg, Sigfather, Hnikud, All-father, Atrid, Farmatyr, Oski ("God of Wishes"), Omi, Just-as-high, Blindi, Gondlir, Harbard, Svidur, Svidrir, Ialk, Kialar, Vidur, Thror, Ygg, Thund, Vakr, Skilfing, Vafud, Hropta-Tyr, Gaut, Veratyr." He is the god of war and battle but also of thought, logic and poetry. He is often referred to as All-father. Described a large man when outside the confines of his hall, he is depicted with a cloak, a staff and a large brimmed hat. This hat is pulled down low to disguise the fact that he only has one eye, as he sacrificed the other at the Well of Urd in order to gain "inner wisdom" which he prized above all things. When riding into battle you see him on his amazing eight-legged steed Sleipnir, with the ever present ravens on his shoulders: Hugin, (thought) and Munin, (memory). He is also accompanied by two wolves; Geri (Greedy) and Freki (Ravenous). He married three times: Fjorgyn, Frigga and Rind. His sons were Thor, Balder, Hoder, Tyr, Bragi, Heimdall, Uil, Hermod, Vidar and Vali. The latter two are destined to survive Ragnarok.

As part of his quest for wisdom, Odin wanted to learn the knowledge and power of the runes. For this he had to wound himself with his own sword, Gungnir, and then hang on Yggdrasil with a noose around his neck for 9 days and nights. Each night he would learn a new secret.

"I know that I hung,

on a wind-rocked tree,

nine whole nights,

with a spear wounded,

and to Odin offered,

myself to myself;

on that tree, of which no one knows

from what root it springs.

Bread no one gave me,

nor a horn of drink,

downward I peered,

to runes applied myself,

wailing learnt them,

then fell down thence."

The tale of Sleipnir, Odin's horse, bears retelling as well. Just after the war between the Vanir and the Æsir, one of the Giants offered to build an impenetrable wall around Asgard over the course of three seasons in order to provide permanent protection to the Æsir. The price he proposed was very high: he wanted the Sun, the Moon, and the Goddess Freya's hand in marriage. The jittery gods wanted the sturdy wall built and, with the proviso that the Giant had to perform the task on his own with the help of just one horse, they agreed, as the Æsir felt it was an impossible task. The Giant's horse, Svaðilfar, was so strong and tireless that he could just as well have been an army to help building the wall. The God's panicked when they saw that the Giant might actually meet the deadline, so they sent Loki (see below) to put a spanner in the works. Loki transformed himself into a mare in heat and led Svaðilfar astray, which prevented the Giant from completing the task. However, Loki found himself with foal; thus was Sleipnir born and gifted to Odin. Inheriting great strength and stamina, Sleipnir was also courageous, noble and extremely fast. He had 8 legs, one for each dimension and direction in heaven, and he was the only steed who could carry his rider to the Land of the Dead and back. His name meant "Gliding" and there is an interesting link to the Vikings in this myth. In about 900 CE, the Vikings imported horses to Iceland from Norway. These horses had 2 extra gaits as well as the normal walk, trot and canter. One was called the Tölt or "running walk" and the other the Flying Pace. This was a "2 beat lateral gait" and is used for racing. An Icelandic horse in action actually looks as if it could have 8 legs as it glides by. "Loki … bore a grey foal with eight legs. This is the horse Sleipnir, which excels all horses ever possessed by gods or men." The great god Odin and his faithful horse Sleipnir came to be inseparable.

Thor was Odin's son and he is somewhat more spectacular in appearance. The god of thunder and lightning, also of the sky, fertility, and law and order, Thor had a bushy, red beard, a huge appetite - and a quick temper, though his bouts of anger would be here and gone in a flash.. He is always depicted with three items in his possession: a magic belt, Megingjard, which doubles his strength; his hammer, called Mjölnir; and the iron gloves he needed to wield the weapon. The mighty iron hammer was forged for him by two dwarves, Sindri and Brokkr, though it is variously depicted as a mallet and sometimes an axe as well as a hammer. It could change size, even fitting inside his tunic if need be, and it always returned to his hand. His chariot was drawn by two goats, Tanngrisni, meaning "gap-toothed", and Tanngnjósrt, meaning "tooth-grinder". Their journeys created thunder, and lightning flashed from a whetstone embedded in Thor's skull. His hall is called Bilskirnir. He married the Goddess Sif – though he kept the goddess Jarnsaxa as his mistress as well. He had two daughters called Magni and Modi and a son called Thrud.

One day the giant king Thrym stole Thor's hammer and demanded the goddess Freya should become his wife in exchange for its return. The gods were not amused and, as they often did, they called upon Loki to devise a plan to get them out of this fix. The gods pretended to acquiesce to the ransom demand, and the day of the marriage was set – and it involved Thor taking Freya's place at the altar. Thor, as you can imagine, was not much impressed with the plan. "Then said Thor, the mighty As: 'Me the Æsir will call womanish, if I let myself be clad in bridal raiment.' The god Loki, not one to mince words, pointed out that Thor's hammer in the hands of the Jotuns could only lead to an unacceptable loss of defensive capabilities to the Æsir and might put the entire Asgard at risk.

A grumpy Thor dressed himself as a splendid bride and Loki made a convincing bridesmaid. At the wedding feast, Thor was in such a bad mood that he ate all the food and drink that had been prepared for the guests. Loki explained that the bride had been so excited prior to the wedding that she had not eaten nor drunk for eight days and that was why she was so very famished. Entranced by this, Thrym peeped under his bride-to-be's veil and was startled by the fierce and fiery eyes that met his gaze. Loki hastened to say that she was feverish with desire for the marriage bed, and that did it for Thrym. He called for the hammer to be brought from its hiding place, eight fathoms under the earth, so that he could swear his marriage vows on it. Mjölnir was laid on the "bride's" lap. "Then said Thrym: 'Bring the hammer in, the bride to consecrate; lay Miollnir on the maiden's knee; unite us each with other by the hand of Vor.' Laughed [Thor's] soul in his breast, when the fierce-hearted his hammer recognized." Thor ripped off his veil and killed all the giants that were at the feast. This is how Thor and Mjölnir were re-united.

Baldur, the Bright One, was another of Odin's sons, one from his marriage to Frigga, and a very different person compared to Thor. He was the God of light, love, reconciliation and radiance, and was very beautiful to behold. He was married to Nanna, the goddess of Joy. It was said that sacred wells sprang up from the hoof marks of his horse. He was goodness and kindness personified, and perhaps a bit of a momma's boy. Frigga experienced disturbing dreams about something terrible happening to Baldur. She then went all around the worlds and made every plant and creature she could find promise not to do anything to harm him. Everyone agreed – everyone, that is, but the Mistletoe, which Frigga did not speak to. It soon became known that Baldur was now impervious to injury and a stupid party trick developed where guests would throw all kinds of odd missiles at him during banquets and laugh as they bounced off him. Loki, the prankster and devious one, made a lethal dart of mistletoe which he took to the next big banquet. He didn't have to wait too long and this silly game was started. Loki sidled up to the blind god Hodur and asked, in an undertone, why he was not joining in the fun. Hodur pointed out that apart from the fact that he had nothing suitable to throw he was not able to see where Baldur was standing. "'Come then,' said Loki, 'do like the rest, and show honour to Baldur by throwing this twig at him, and I will direct thy arm, toward the place where he stands.'" The trusting Hodur then threw the Mistletoe dart, allowing his hand to be guided by the willy Loki - aided by his excellent hearing, Hodur hit the mark and Baldur was "pierced through and through, [and] fell down lifeless." The Gods were stunned at this turn of events and in the uproar as a consequence of this atrocious deed, Loki just slipped away and went on the run.

Loki is surely the most puzzling of the Norse gods. He was neither an Æsir nor a Vanir but was of the race of elementals called Etins and was originally their God of Fire. He was actually the son of a Giant but he tricked his way into becoming Odin's blood brother. He was known as a Shapeshifter, a Trickster, the "Sky Traveler", and the "Father-of-Lies". He married Glut (Glow), who bore him two daughters; Eisa (Embers) and Einmyria (Ashes). He also coupled with the Giantess Angr-boda and produced three monsters: Hel, the Goddess of the Dead; Jormungand, the great serpent who encircles Midgard; and Fenrir or Fenris the Wolf. With his third wife, Sigyn, he had two children, Vali and Narfi, who would later have a hand in his capture. He was good-looking, charming, ingenious and amoral and his pranks often had a twist of viciousness. On the other hand, the Gods often called on him to get them out of tight spots. The killing of Baldur was however a "prank" that had gone too far, and the Æsir set about to capture him. After many evasions they eventually trapped him in a cave. Vali and Narfi were also captured and the Gods turned Vali into a wolf who attacked and tore his brother, Narfi, apart. Narfi's entrails were used to bind Loki to three flat, heavy stones: one around his chest, one around his loins, and one around his knees – these entrails then turned into iron. Skadi, the goddess of Wintertime Havoc who leads the Wild Hunt and who holds wolves and venomous snakes sacred, and the one after whom Scandinavia is named, then fastened such a snake over Loki's head so that it would drip venom onto his face. Sigyn was allowed to sit with him holding a bowl over Loki's head, to collect the venom. Unfortunately, when she leaves him to empty the bowl, the venom drops into his eyes. This causes Loki to shudder violently, triggering an earthquake so severe that torments mankind: "But while she [Sigyn] is doing this, venom falls upon Loki, which makes him howl with horror, and twist his body about so violently that the whole earth shakes, and this produces what men call earthquakes." Nevertheless, Loki is destined to lie there in chains until Ragnarok.

Freya is the most beautiful Norse goddess. She presides over love, fertility, lust, war, battle, wealth and death, so it will not surprise you to know that she also leads the Valkyries. The cat is her sacred animal and her chariot is drawn by two cats, though sometimes she is shown riding a boar. She was initially married to a mysterious god called Od who suddenly left her and subsequently disappeared. This caused her to shed tears of red gold. She practiced a form of Norse magic called seiðr and she had a special magic cloak of falcon feathers which allowed her to turn into a bird. She is usually depicted wearing an exquisite necklace called Brisingamen. This was wrought for her specifically by four dwarves. The price she paid was to spend one night with each dwarf. Loki (who else?) ran to Odin with this scandal and the All-father ordered Loki to steal the necklace from her. This was a lot easier said than done as getting into Freya's well guarded hall, Sessrumnir, was difficult and called for much shape shifting on Odin's part. First he had to turn himself into a fly to get through a crack in the fortress and then, finding her asleep wearing the necklace, with her chin concealing the clasp, he had to turn into a flea and bite her on the opposite cheek. As she turned her head in her sleep, he was able to unclasp Brisingamen and flee in his own guise. Odin refused to return the necklace to Freya until she had stirred up war among human beings.

One of the less attractive things about Odin, who was her lover, was that he spent a great deal of his time stirring up war and discontent. This was to produce as many heroic warriors as possible to fight on the God's side at Ragnarok. Freya, with the other Valkyries, watched over all war and battles. They selected the fighters who would live and who would die.

Freyr was Freya's twin brother and he was the horned god of fertility - also the god of sun, rain, harvests and prosperity as well as the protector of ships. He rides a golden boar called Gullenbarsti and he commands a magical ship, Skidbladnir, which always sails in the right direction, can never sink, and can change shape and size to fit in his pocket. He is the ruler of the Light Elves in Alfheimr, who were the ones that built Skidbladnir with a combination of skill, ingenuity and sorcery. She was large enough to accommodate all the Æsir with their weapons and war stores and equipped with the equivalent of an Elven Norse GPS so that she never became lost at sea. "As soon as the sails are set a favourable breeze arises and carries her to her place of destination, and she is made of so many pieces, and with so much skill, that when she is not wanted for a voyage Frey may fold her together like a piece of cloth, and put her in his pocket." Skidbladnir had one other fabulous attribute: she could sail on the sea, in the air and over land. Freyr is said to be an ancestor of the Yngling family who once ruled what is now Scandinavia.

Chapter Four

Valhalla

"Five hundred doors

And forty more

Methinks are in Valhalla.

Eight hundred heroes through each door

Shall issue forth

Against the wolf to combat."

"A wolf hangs before the western door,

over it an eagle hovers."

It is now time to talk about Valhalla, the Hall of the Battle Slain. This was the mythical place that inspired the most intrepid adventurers of the past, the Vikings, to hurl themselves into the most perilous journeys in uncharted waters and land on unknown shores, armed only with their swords, armor made of boar skin, and their lust for life, to protect them. Each warrior believed that the only proper way to die was in doing heroic deeds in battle. Those who fell would be swept up and carried on horseback by the Valkyrie, either to Valhalla, to dwell with Odin, or to Fólkvangr to dwell with Freya. There is some dissention about the exact location of Valhalla. Most sources place it in Asgard but there is a body of evidence that indicates that it might be elsewhere, perhaps even in Helheim! However all agree on what happens there. Odin certainly presides and the heroes' wounds are healed; they live there forevermore, improving on their battle skills, feasting on meat and mead until the call to the great battle of Ragnarok – the end of the world. These heroes were known as Einherjar.

Chapter Five

Ragnarok

Ragnarok is the predestined end of the cycle of Norse mythology. It is for this great and final battle, which they know they will lose, that all the warrior gods, aided by the valiant human and mythical heroes from Valhalla, have lived and died and will die again. There will be signs which oddly enough will first manifest in Midgard. Human bonds of kinship as well as traditional beliefs will shrivel and disappear. A listless anarchy will evolve. Then there will be a period of time known as Fimbulvetr, characterized by three winters of increasing severity with no summers in between. Three roosters will crow: the crimson rooster Fjalar will crow to the Giants; the golden cock Gullinkambi will crow to the gods; and a third cock will raise the dead. The sun will be devoured by the wolf, Skoll, and his brother, Hati, will eat the moon leaving the world in darkness. Earthquakes will set Fenrir the Great Wolf free and he will open his mouth so wide that his upper jaw captures heaven and his lower jaw the Earth, and he will rampage through all the nine worlds, destroying all that lives. Great mountains will fall in on their foundations. The seas will overrun the land as the serpent Jormungand comes ashore. "On the waters floats the ship Naglfar, which is constructed of the nails of dead men. For which reason great care should be taken to die with pared nails, for he who dies with his nails unpared, supplies materials for the building of this vessel, which both gods and men wish may be finished as late as possible. But in this flood shall Naglfar float, and the giant Hrym be its steersman". A second ship from Hel will set sail with Loki at the helm and the Fire Giants, led by the God Surt, will head for the battlefield, scorching the earth as they march.

Then will the one who guards Bifrost, the beautiful Heimdall, sound his horn. Odin, All-father, will rally his warriors and head for the battle plain of Vigrid. First Odin will ride to Mimir's Well to consult other Gods on a suitable battle plan. Yggdrasil the great Cosmic Tree will start to shake, and that will bring fear into every heart, even the most brave, as this will signal that Ragnarok is upon them. "The Æsir and all the heroes of Valhalla arm themselves and speed forth to the field, led on by Odin, with his golden helm and resplendent cuirass, and his spear called Gungnir." Much ferocious hand to hand battle will take place: Thor will defeat the serpent; Baldur will really be killed by Loki; Heimdall will kill Loki; Surt will defeat Freyr. Odin dies fighting Fenrir, who swallows him whole. "After this, Surtur darts fire and flame over the earth, and the whole universe is consumed." It then sinks into the sea, creating another Ginnunngagap. This initiates another cycle of the Myth and it is this cyclical nature of the story which makes it so very different from the Christian version of the creation which has a very linear structure.

Chapter Six

The Sagas

The word "saga" comes from the Old Norse and means "that which is told". It is entirely an oral tradition. While the most common definition of a saga is a medieval, Icelandic or Norse prose narrative of achievements and events in the history of a person or family, a second definition broadens the scope to what is more widely accepted today: North or Scandinavian mythology. The history of North Germanic people, stemming from Norse paganism and continuing after the Christianization of Scandinavia and into the folklore of modern time.

Originally the sagas were retold by the elders of the community or the professional Skalds as they travelled around the country. The setting for these tales to be told could be the warm, family longhouse on a bitterly cold, long winter night or the splendiferous banquet hall of a great king. This storytelling was taken very seriously as it commemorated and extended the history of the various tribes and instilled the necessary faith and proper goals to strive for among the young. Being a skilled poet and Skald was a big deal as can be demonstrated in the life of Egill Skallagrimsson, a poet, warrior and slaughterer of many men as well as an Icelandic farmer. His frank tales and sagas put him on the wrong side of Erik Blood-Axe, sometime king of Norway, who eventually grew impatient with his actual crimes and endless impudence, arrested him, and sentenced him to death in the morning. Egill spent the night composing an epic poem called the Höfuðlausn. (Head-Ransom) He was allowed to recite the poem the next morning before his execution and the Blood-Axe was so moved by the power and the beauty of the poem that he forgave Egill for all his wrongdoing. Here is a brief extract:

"The scream of swords,

The clash of shields,

These are true words

On battlefields:

Man sees his death

Frozen in dreams,

But Eirik's breath

Frees battle-streams.

The war-lord weaves

His web of fear,

Each man receives

His fated share:

A blood-red sun's

The warrior's shield,

The eagle scans

The battlefield.

As edges swing,

Blades cut men down.

Eirik the King

Earns his renown."

This is a translation of the poem by Hermann Palsson and Paul Edwards for Penguin. You can read the entire poem online at: http://www.odins-gift.com/pclass/hoefudlausn.htm. This legend might seem farfetched, especially when you look at the elemental and conflict prone lives of the people of the time. However, the gift of poetry was highly regarded; the rules of composition were extremely taxing and the play on words and ingenuity of plot a matter for serious consideration. It is not an exaggeration to say that verbal battles could be as treacherous and dangerous as a battle on the field and the rewards and losses similarly consequential.

The sagas dealt with fate, luck, honour, the supernatural and prophecy. Always in the background was the eternal quandary of good against evil. The Norse people believed in predestination and did not feel it was important to explain people's actions as "each must do as destiny decides." Life was full of epic blood feuds. The themes taught the importance of protecting the household and homestead, competition with "outsiders", and the danger of treachery and trickery. The sagas were filled with doom and gloom but "laced with gleams of grandeur and sparks of humour". Tales of heroism abounded and the heroes and gods were required to accept their fate and destiny with reckless disregard. The traits of the heroic warrior were courage, honour and generosity. Society in medieval Iceland made little distinction between the sexes, particularly in their storytelling. People were not divided by their gender but by how physically able and skilled they were. The tales were full of powerful matriarchs, faithful and faithless wives and trouble-stirring females. The subjects could be historical or legendary and were full of mythical and mystical animals, signs and numbers.

The number nine for example occurs over and over again. During Ragnarok, the god Thor battles with the serpent Jormungand and in fact kills him. Thor steps away as his foe falls, but after taking nine steps, he falls to the ground. He struggles to his feet and takes another nine steps, but again he falls to the ground. He repeats this a total of nine times as the poison the serpent spat at him during the epic battle inexorably overcomes his system; in the end the great Thor rises no more.

Another example of this is the story of how two dwarfs, Brokk and Sindri, fashion an exquisite golden ring for Odin called Draupnir. On every ninth day, Draupnir would produce eight new rings. Additionally, In his desire to learn the secret of the runes, Odin hung on the tree Yggdrasil for nine days, with a noose around his neck, without food, drink or comfort, learning one of nine mighty spells each night.

In the heyday of Viking pillaging along the coasts of Britain, the marauders would often kidnap young men as slaves and hostages and sail away with them. If the seas became very rough and the ship was in danger, every tenth hostage might be thrown overboard as an appeasing sacrifice to the sea Gods.

Another popular saga tells of the Wild Hunt; Furious Host or Raging Host – the Asgardsreien. It starts on 31 October and spectral horsemen and horsewomen led by Frigga and Odin on Sleipnir his great eight-legged steed can be seen racing across the winter sky in company with the Valkyrie and the fallen warriors in training from Valhalla. The sounds are earth shattering: blaring horns calling the howling hounds, thundering hooves and raging winds sweeping through the still, cold night. The peak of the hunt happens on Yuletide and the furious ride ends on Walpurgis Night on the 30th of April. All the light in the nine worlds is extinguished and all the spirits of the newly dead can roam freely to celebrate the final day of winter. It usually has evil connotations as a time when wicked witches consort with devils, but this is one of the many pagan rites that have been "cleaned-up" and adapted to the Christian liturgical calendar as All Soul's Day, when the dead are honoured.

There is an amazing online source for all the sagas at: http://sagadb.org/

Chapter Seven

The Influence of Norse Mythology on Our Lives Today

The naming of the days of the week is heavily influenced by Norse and Germanic mythology. Sunday is named for the Goddess of the Sun, Sol. She is pulled around the earth by her two fine horses. They are chased by the monstrous wolf, Skoll, who occasionally manages to snap at her ankles, thus producing a solar eclipse. Monday is named for her brother, Mani. His horse-drawn chariot is also pursued by the giant wolf, Hati. When he almost catches up, there is a lunar eclipse. Tuesday is named for Tyr, the God of war and justice. A difficult portfolio to balance, even then. Wednesday was actually named for the Germanic God, Wodan, who is the equivalent of Odin, the All-father. Thursday is named for Thor, the God of thunder. He is probably the Norse god we all know the most about because he made it to the comic books and graphic novels big time! Friday is actually named after the Roman goddess Venus; the Norse connection is that Venus was known as Frigga's star. Frigga was a complex goddess, as she actually knew the fate of everyone, even after Ragnarok, but she never revealed it. Saturday was named for the planet Saturn. In Roman mythology Saturn was the god of agriculture. In the Norse pantheon there isn't a direct correlation as many of the gods and goddesses are associated with fertility, farming and harvesting, so it is the only name of a day of the week that does not have a particularly Norse connection.

There are many social traditions, especially around Christian religious events, that harken back to Norse mythology: Yule logs, Christmas trees, decorating eggs at Easter time are only a few. Perhaps Santa Claus driving his reindeer through the sky is an echo of the Wild Hunt. There is one story that mentions the tradition of leaving a sack of hay out for Sleipnir during this time. Perhaps this evolved into leaving a plate of cookies and milk or beer for Santa?

Norse Runes

In an overwhelmingly oral tradition it is perhaps odd that runes receive so much attention. What is a "rune"? The word means a "mystery or a secret" perhaps even a "whisper". It is a unique symbol representing a letter in the Old Norse alphabet. They were used for writing, as protection, divination or "rune casting" and casting spells. There are three variations called "futharks" and the oldest dates back to 100 BCE. The god Odin was so intent on increasing his wisdom that he went to great lengths to gain the knowledge and the power of the runes. He is said to have passed this knowledge on to Freya, who then taught Heimdall, he who guards the Rainbow Bridge. Heimdall taught the runes to the human race. Apart from representing a single letter, each and every rune has a group of specific meanings attached to it and if it falls, or is written "reversed" or "merkstave", it takes on a negative connotation. Here are a few examples:

M (pronounced manaz). Overall meaning = man or mankind. It signifies: The Self; the individual or the human race. Your attitude toward others and their attitudes towards you. Friends and enemies, social order. Intelligence, forethought, creativity, skill, ability. Divine structure, intelligence, awareness. Expect to receive some sort of aid or cooperation now. Mannaz Reversed or Merkstave: Depression, mortality, blindness, self-delusion. Cunning, slyness, manipulation, craftiness, calculation. Expect no help now.

R (pronounced raidho). Overall meaning = wagon or chariot. It signifies: Travel, both in physical terms and those of lifestyle direction. A journey, vacation, relocation, evolution, change of place or setting. Seeing a wider perspective. Seeing the right move for you to make and deciding upon it. Personal rhythm, world rhythm, the dance of life. Raidho Reversed or Merkstave: Crisis, rigidity, stasis, injustice, irrationality. Disruption, dislocation, demotion, delusion, possibly a death.

I (pronounced isa). Overall meaning = ice. It signifies: A challenge or frustration. Psychological blocks to thought or activity, including grievances. Standing still, or a time to turn inwards and wait for what is to come, or to seek clarity. This rune reinforces runes around it. Isa Merkstave (Isa cannot be reversed, but may lie in opposition): Ego-mania, dullness, blindness, dissipation. Treachery, illusion, deceit, betrayal, guile, stealth, ambush, plots.

I would like to acknowledge my indebtedness to Ingrid Halvorsen's exceptional website called: Runes, Alphabet of Mystery for the details of the runic alphabet. It can be found at: http://sunnyway.com/runes/

Runic symbols were often used as protection on possessions, particularly weapons. Swords, shields, spears and knives might have a Tiwaz rune engraved on the handle to ensure victory in battle. Runes were also used as decorative motifs on finely wrought containers for precious objects or in wood carvings. The symbols were made up exclusively of straight lines or edges to facilitate carving. In the extremely wealthy households the drinking vessels, plates, cutlery, and linen might also have runic monograms. Certainly the letters with their particular meanings formed the basis for jewelry design and decoration on works of art, like vases. The use of runes in jewelry design is one of the most beautiful influences of Norse ancestry that prevails today. Modern body painting and serious tattoo artists owe much of their inspiration to Norse designs.

In terms of literature, Norse mythology was the inspiration for the brilliant fantasy novels The Hobbit and Lord of the Rings trilogy by JRR Tolkien and surely also played a part in the Harry Potter books by J K Rowling. Music too, particularly opera, would be much poorer if Richard Wagner had not submerged himself in his Nordic heritage and produced that thrilling, stupendous and lushly orchestrated score for Der Ring des Nibelungen. Edvard Grieg also composed a fabulous score for his opera about Olaf Trygvason in 1870. Norse mythology has also been popularized by Marvel comics, movies and video games, pinball machines in gaming arcades and of course computer games, not to mention in strategy games in management training.

Religious Influences

The influence of Norse mythology is even more visible today in a revival of interest in "heathenry", particularly in Scandinavia, Iceland and the United States of America. This revival has "the aim of forming a faith tradition that is deeply rooted in the ancient past, and yet can speak to the needs and concerns of modern people". (Stephan Grundy, 2015. God in Flames, God in Fetters: Loki's role in the Northern Religions. Lulu.com. page vi). This interest has taken various forms:

• Theodism. A religious movement started in 1976 by Garman Lord. He looks for historical accuracy in how he follows the old gods. This is not a matter of simply duplicating rituals etc but of truly contextualizing old teachings and being able to apply the principles to the modern world. The concept of tribalism and hierarchy are an important part of re-developing this way of living.

• Wicca. Wicca beliefs are more rooted in Celtic than Germanic paganism but there are similarities mainly in the strong influence of the belief in gods, goddesses and nature worship. "Wiccan practice involves the manipulation of nature through various rituals in attempts to gain power, prestige, love, or whatever else a Wiccan wants." (Christian Apologetics & Research

Ministry. https://carm.org/) There is a committed belief in re-incarnation and karma.

- **Asatru.** Asatru is probably the most important modern pagan religion today. The word means "belief in the gods" and it is expanding steadily in the United Kingdom, France, USA, South Africa, Europe and particularly in Scandinavia. It was formally founded by a sheep farmer in Iceland called Sveinbjorn Beinteinsson (1924 – 1993). In 1945 he published a book of Icelandic rhymed poetry. He had a wonderfully sonorous voice and the physical appearance of an ancient skald. He made regular public appearances reading his own poems and reciting the sagas from the Eddas. He has also made many recordings, some of which can be found on YouTube today. In 1972 he petitioned the Icelandic government to recognize Islenska Ásatrúarfélagið as an Icelandic, neopagan, congregation of faith, with the purpose of reviving the pre-Christianization religion of Scandinavia. It was officially recognized as a national religion in 1973 in Iceland – followed shortly by Denmark and Norway.

The present allsherjargooi, (priest) is Hilmar Orn Hilmarsson. In 2015, the members opened the very first modern temple to the Norse gods that has ever been built. It is located in Pingvellir National Park, near Reykjavik. Asatru communities are called "Kindreds" and the meetings are called "Blots" which means "sacrifice". Mead, which is a honeyed wine, beer or cider, is consecrated to a particular god and, after everyone has taken a drink, the rest is poured out as a libation to that god. One variation of this ritual is a Sumbel which is a toast in three rounds. The first toast is to Odin; the second toast is to the ancestors and the honorable dead; and the third toast is open to anyone. The followers are committed to the Nine Noble Virtues: Courage, Truth, Honour, Fidelity, Discipline, Hospitality, Industriousness, Self-reliance, and Perseverance. One should live one's life with due regard to these virtues and, if you succeed, you will go on in the afterlife to "greater fulfillment, pleasure and challenge". If one lives badly, you will be "separated from your kin and live in dullness and gloom" in your afterlife. The movement is growing steadily and earning more official recognition every day. Recently the US Army and Air Force has added "Heathen" and "Asatru" to the Religious Preferences list their recruits are required to fill in to describe their religion.

• **Asatru Folk Assembly** is an off-shoot of the initial group in the USA, the Asatru Free Assembly, and was formed by Stephen McNallen in 1994 as a result of dissention about neo-Nazi membership. Membership to the AFA is based on bloodlines and although they deny any hint of racism in their practices, they only welcome people of proven Germanic descent. To quote McNallen: "One of the most controversial tenets of Asatru is our insistence that ancestry matters- that there are spiritual and metaphysical implications to heredity, and that we are thus a religion not for all of humanity, but rather one that calls only its own."

• **The Odin Brotherhood** is a version of Asatru and they call themselves "a secret society for men and women who value "knowledge, freedom, and power." You can find out more about them online at:http://www.odinbrotherhood.com/

Conclusion

Let us return to our main source, the Eddas. One of the many startling issues one has to come to terms with as one delves into Norse mythology is this concept of the cyclical as opposed to the linear. What happens after Ragnarok? We are told that the cycle just begins again but, we are also told that two human beings, Lif and Lifthrasir, actually survive Ragnarok by hiding in the trunk of the cosmic tree, so that already makes a difference. "Thou must know, moreover, that during the conflagration caused by Surtur's fire, a woman named Lif (Life), and a man named Lifthrasir, lie concealed in Hodmimir's forest. They shall feed on morning dew, and their descendants shall soon spread over the whole earth."

The Eddas explain that several Gods do survive and that they meet in Idavoll, which is a beautiful, verdant meadow, where Asgard used to be, and they start to build an even more splendid dwelling called Gimli; this time with a roof of gold rather than silver. They mention two other heavens where the dead will rest in peace as well as a dreadful place called Nastrond; cold and completely devoid of sunlight where "oath breakers, murderers, and philanderers" will roam. The worst place though is Hvergelmir, where Nidhog, the dragon who survived Ragnarok, will suck out the blood and "bedevil the bodies of the dead".

Essentially the world will be a better place, where the gods and the giants actually live in harmony and humans will not be afflicted by wickedness and misery. So, perhaps each cycle represents a reincarnation, a growth of the soul, gained with difficulty, to be fit to live with God. This idea is not in conflict with Norse mythology, as there are many instances of being "re-born", "re-made", or transmigrated into another form. A final quote from the Eddas:

"And now…if thou hast any further questions to ask, I know not who can answer thee, for I never heard tell of any one who could relate what will happen in the other ages of the world. Make, therefore, the best use thou canst of what has been imparted to thee."

EGYPTIAN MYTHOLOGY

A Concise Guide to the Ancient Gods and Beliefs of Egyptian Mythology

"As a camel beareth labour, and heat, and hunger and thirst, through deserts of sand, and fainteth not; so the fortitude of man shall sustain him through all perils."

Pharaoh Akhenaton, 18th dynasty

Introduction

The particular geography of Egypt has played a critical role in its history. This can be said of many countries of course, but in Egypt it seems to have had an "undue influence" on its development. A thin land, it is bracketed by Libya and the immense Sahara in the west and the Red Sea, Jordan and Saudi Arabia in the east. In the north it is fringed by the Mediterranean. Unlike in most ancient countries, the people of Egypt, from time immemorial, have been oriented to the north. There lies the main fascination for Egyptians, the immense river of life, the Nile, that flows from the south and divides the full length of Egypt into two unequal land masses. Known as "the gift of Egypt", the Nile is what made life possible in this otherwise arid land, and it has always supported the existence, development, abundance and mystique of this enduring country. The subject of this publication, Egyptian mythology, has been defined as follows: the belief structure and underlying form of ancient Egyptian culture from circa 3500 BCE to circa 30 BCE.

It is a fascinating and complex story and to appreciate it fully you should refer to the timeline in the next section as you read. More than in other mythologies, the distinction between immortal God and human being was extremely tenuous to the Egyptians; sometimes the characters that populate the story are both an historical human being and a mythological god. The Gods do not dwell in the sky above, as in most other mythologies, but in manmade temples during their lives and then in giant pyramids when they move into the Underworld. For this reason it is essential that in exploring the mythology you should have a reasonable understanding of the real history of the country.

Chapter One

A Timeline for Ancient Egypt

I will make this as brief as possible and only highlight key events. You may even want to skip this section at this point and refer back when you need to orient yourself in the history. Prior to this timeline, Egypt was divided in two: Upper Egypt, represented by a white crown; and Lower Egypt, represented by a Red Crown. Upper Egypt stretched south towards the source of the Nile and was characterized by the desert. Lower Egypt stretched north and was characterized by the rich and fertile land of the Nile Delta, where the mighty river fanned out into many smaller waterways running to the sea. In the Pre-dynastic period, the north defeated the south and the land was united under King Menes, who thereafter wore a double crown to signify the unification. The truth is lost in the mists of time, but of King Menes it has been said that he inherited the throne from the falcon-headed God Horus; he may actually have been the mythical Narmer or Aha; he was the first pharaoh of the first dynasty; and that he ruled circa 3407 to circa 3368 BCE. What does seem to be uncontested fact is that he united Egypt and it is here that we start the timeline.

EARLY DYNASTIC PERIOD c3159 – 2686BCE

1ST AND 2ND DYNASTY

Menes united Upper and Lower Egypt and established Memphis as the capital. This gave him control over the agricultural produce of the Delta and the expanding Levant trading routes. The wealth, influence and power of the pharaohs was established and the rituals and cults around the burial tombs, the mastaba, were inculcated among the population.

THE OLD KINGDOM c2686 – 2181BCE

3RD TO 6TH DYNASTY

The centralized administration supported major developments in several areas. The Great Sphinx and the three Giza pyramids were constructed. Imhotep, a gifted architect, was born in 2667 BCE and was influential to his death in 2600 BCE and beyond. There were developments in medicine, mathematics, literature and technology; for example the development of the ceramic glaze known as faience occurred during this period. A combination of factors brought this productive time to an end; the administration became top-heavy; central authority was challenged from smaller centers and a crippling drought developed from c2200 BCE.

FIRST INTERMEDIATE PERIOD c2181 – 2040BCE

7TH TO MIDWAY THROUGH THE 11TH DYNASTY

Regional governors became less dependent on the pharaohs as provincial areas initially thrived and prospered. As individual families became economically and culturally richer, the inevitable rivalries for political power and land ownership escalated and eventually Lower Egypt was controlled by rulers in Herakleopolis and Upper Egypt was claimed by the Intef clan based in Thebes. Around 2055 BCE a victory by the Theban forces imposed unity again and the destructive era drew to a close. Recent research has revealed that the annual flooding of the Nile was less pronounced during this period.

MIDDLE KINGDOM c2040 – 1786BCE

END OF 11TH AND 12TH DYNASTY

The return of the power of the pharaohs, ruling from Thebes, reinforced former glory and traditions. Senusret l built the largest temple ever at Karnak in honor of Anum-Re. In what has been called a "democratization of the afterlife" the ordinary population also followed more lavish and ritualized burial procedures; there was also a general increase in religious observance. The pharaohs of the 12th dynasty were quite far-sighted - instead of relying on the annual flooding of the Nile, they began supportive irrigation schemes and extensive reclamation of land, impressively improving the agricultural output. Works started on building a dam to control the flow of water into the Faiyum Depression at Lahum by Pharaoh Senusert ll. Needing more laborers, Amenemhat lll allowed Asiatic settlers into the Delta areas. They also re-conquered land lost in Nubia, including much needed quarries and gold mines. As this golden age drew to a close, inadequate Nile flooding and a strained economy produced tensions and political upheaval; the "settlers" took control of the Delta region and came to power in Egypt as the Hykos.

SECOND INTERMEDIATE PERIOD c1786 – 1567BCE

13TH TO 17TH DYNASTY

This was a period of foreign control in Egypt. The pharaohs were pushed back to Thebes and were harassed by the Hykos, both in the north and by their Nubian allies the Kushites in the south. A war of resistance went on for thirty years until the Hykos were finally defeated by Ahmose l.

THE NEW KINGDOM c1567 – 1069BCE

18TH TO 20TH DYNASTY

Initially, under the military, this was a time of increasing prosperity as Egypt expanded its territory. The Pharaohs Tuthmosis l and ll gradually reintroduced traditional beliefs and supported the influence of the Amun Priests. In 1350 BCE there began an unprecedented upheaval when Amenhotep lV ascended the throne. A devotee of the rather obscure sun-disc God Aten, he promoted the following of Aten to the exclusion off any other God for more than twenty years. He changed his name to Akhenaten and built a new Egyptian capital at Amarna, called Akhetaten. This became known as the Amarna Heresy and it caused much dismay and chaos; Akhenaten even went as far as ordering the destruction of certain temples dedicated to other gods.

The situation was salvaged by the coming of Ramesses ll, known as Ramesses the Great, to the throne in 1279 BCE. Once again the people were encouraged to honor all the gods and to have freedom of choice in terms of who they followed. Ramesses the Great steadily increased the wealth of Egypt by successful military campaigns. He is also credited with making the first written peace treaty ever recorded, which was signed with the Hittites in 1258B CE after both sides acknowledged a stalemate in the wake of the Battle of Kardesh. The immense accumulation of wealth led to increasing invasions from external enemies. There were also increasing domestic problems with corruption, tomb robbery and civil unrest as this period drew to an uneasy close. This would possibly have been the period of the biblical ten Plagues of Egypt, according to Michael Oblath's article "Route of Exodus". (2007 Sakenfeld, KD ed. The New Interpreter's Dictionary of the Bible, vol 2, Nashville, Abingdon Press.)

THIRD INTERMEDIATE PERIOD c1069 - 664BCE

21ST TO 25TH DYNASTY

Once again Egypt lost the unity which made her strong. The nation fractured, with Smendes ll the power in the north and the Priests of Amun at Thebes holding sway in the south, barely paying lip service to the pharaoh. There had been an increase of Libyans settling in the Delta and under Shoshenq l, an influx of Libyan princes created what is termed the Bubastite dynasty, which lasted for about 200 years. Their power was broken by an invasion by the Kushite King Piye in c727 BCE, setting the stage for the 25th dynasty – a veritable renaissance of old glories and a reunited empire. Great monuments, including many temples, were built or restored, including the construction of the first pyramids in the Nile Valley since the Middle Kingdom.

However, an old enemy lurked in the shadows. In 671 BCE, the Assyrians began an attack that resulted in constant conflict until the Assyrians, having forced the Kushites out, occupied Memphis and sacked the temples at Thebes.

LATE DYNASTIC PERIOD c664 – 332BCE

26TH – 31ST DYNASTY

After their conquest the Assyrians did not show much interest in their prize and left vassals in charge. These were the Saite kings who allowed increasing Greek influence and expansion into Egypt. This was followed by even more interest from Persia, which actually annexed Egypt from the 27th dynasty. The last indigenous royal house of Egypt ended with King Nectanabo ll and in 332 BCE Persia handed Egypt to Alexander the Great without a whimper. Although he was Greek, Alexander was declared a demigod by the Oracle at Siwa. When he died, his place was taken by his favorite general, Ptolemy.

PTOLEMAIC DYNASTY c332 – 30BCE

This period was named for the Greek general, Ptolemy l (305- 284 BCE). It was Ptolemy who started the great library at Alexandria; his successor, Ptolemy ll, completed its construction. The library was said to hold 70,000 papyrus scrolls and eventually 500,000 early books. Alexandria soon supplanted Memphis as the capital of Egypt and the lighthouse that was built there was one of the seven wonders of the ancient world. The Ptolemaic dynasty did support traditional Egyptian culture, but there was some merging with the Greek pantheon. An example of this was the temple built for the Greek god Serapis.

Egypt was conquered by Rome after the Battle of Actium in 30 BCE, where Marc Anthony and Cleopatra Vll were defeated. The Romans were perhaps less well disposed towards the Egyptians, but all their traditions, including mummification, were tolerated even after the advent of Christianity. It was only in 391 CE that Emperor Theodosius banned any and all pagan rites and closed all the temples. Several were turned into churches but most returned gently, quietly and silently to the sands from which they had come and the gods to whom they had been consecrated.

Oh Light ! let the Light be kindled for thy Ka, O Osiris
Chentamenta. Let the Light be kindled for the Night
which
followeth the Day : the Eye of Horus which riseth at thy
temple:
which riseth up over thee and which gathereth upon
thy brow ;
which granteth thee its protection and overthroweth
thine enemies.
Book of the Dead. Spell 275

Chapter Two

Historical Egypt

The Nile: the Egyptians called it "Ar",or "Aur", which meant "black", or "Kemet"; the Black Land or "Ta mery"; the Beautiful One – but mostly they referred to it simply as "the river". It was the Greeks who actually gave the Nile its name, from the word for "valley" i.e. Neilos. The White

Nile rises in Lake Victoria in Equatorial Africa, joins the Blue Nile, which rises at Lake Tana in Ethiopia and snakes its way down to enter Egypt in the south, at Aswan. From there it sweeps down to the Mediterranean Sea. In historical times it had three phases: Akhet, from June to September, when it was in flood, called the inundation; Peret, from October to February, when all the planting for the year took place; and Shemu, from March to May, when the harvesting was done.

When the river receded after the inundation it left a thick, black layer of incredibly fertile silt – black gold which was planted with emmer wheat for bread and barley for beer, the staple foods. Flax plants to spin for linen and papyrus for many products, including paper, baskets and even small boats, were also economically important. Sugarcane, melons, squashes, pulses, lettuce, leeks, garlic and grapes were also successfully cultivated. There was plenty of land as the river was normally about 2 miles wide; during inundation, it could be anything from 5 to 10 miles across! One could get from Aswan to Alexandria in two weeks by Nile while it was in flood – in the dry season, it would take two months.

Society was very stratified but all were equal before the law. Women had equal rights to men. The bulk of the population were farmers but the land they farmed usually belonged to the local temple. They were paid an average of 5 ½ sacks of grain per month, while a foreman might earn 7 ½ half sacks a month. There was no coinage until the late period, and the size of the grain sack was standardized to facilitate bartering. A standard sack of grain was worth a deben, the equivalent of ninety one grams (3 oz.) of copper or silver. A shirt might cost 5 deben or a cow, 40 deben. The above is just to give you a sense of the times; the bartering system was actually extremely complicated, varied over time and place, and suggests that the working population was generally very poor.

The progress of settlement was dictated by the Nile. Many smaller settlements developed along the length of the river rather than large centers as in other countries. In pre-dynasty and Old Kingdom years, Memphis played the role of the de facto capital; in the 11th and18th dynasty Thebes played this part, except for a brief period of twenty years when it was at Akhetaten, and in 331 BCE, Alexandria gained and retained the title of capital. In the historical time we are looking at, the real life of the country was played out in the many towns and villages strung along the banks of "the river".

Apart from supplying the water and soil for agriculture, the Nile was also the single greatest source of transportation. Egypt was rich in natural resources; beautiful decorative stones like sandstone, granite and quartz; gold and lead ore; mineral deposits like flint; clay from the river; salt and precious stones like emeralds and amethysts; all these commodities as well as the huge building stones required for the many temples, monuments, tombs and pyramids were shipped up and down the river on flat barges. Egypt was usually able to export grain, gold, linen and papyrus products, the bulk of which would be moved on the river. Richly endowed as it was, Egypt had to import vast quantities of wood, which was shipped along the length of the river. It also imported the very popular blue stone known as lapis lazuli from Afghanistan as well as olive oil, which had to be distributed to all the settlements along the Nile. As you will discern from the timeline above, Egypt prospered during the more or less centralized Old, Middle and New Kingdoms and did less well during the Intermediate times. Additionally, from about 130 BCE Egypt was an important part of the Silk Road, the trade routes established during the Han dynasty in China, and no longer the isolated, insular and inward-looking country of the early dynastic times.

Chapter Three

The Myth Of Creation

"I am Osiris, the possessor of Maat,

and I subsist by means of it every day."

Book of the Dead

Now the stage is set to look at Egyptian mythology. Where better to start than at the beginning: the creation of all that is. There are several versions, but all contain most of the elements that occur in this version from the Ennead of Heliopolis Cult. In the beginning there were the dark, swirling waters of chaos called Nu. A mound of land called the Ben Ben rose slowly out of the depth and a god stood upon it. In many versions this was Atum; in some it was Ptah. The god felt his "aloneness" and he mated with his shadow, producing two children. He coughed or spat out Shu, the God of Air (or Wind) and vomited up Tefnut the Goddess of Moisture (or Rain). Atum taught Shu the principles of life and Tefnut learned the principles of order. Shu and Tefnut set out to make the rest of the physical world. Atum was left on Ben Ben contemplating the surrounding chaos. After a while he became concerned for his children and he sent his one eye to find them. When they returned, with his eye, he was so overjoyed he started crying with gratitude; human beings manifested from his tears.

There are two versions of the creation of the earth and the sky. In the first, Shu and Tefnut mate to produce Geb, God of the Earth and Nut, Goddess of the Sky. Shu lifts Nut up and she stretches her body over Geb, forming a beautiful, star-filled canopy over him. In the second version, Geb and Nut also fall in love and mate, but because they are natural brother and sister, Atum is not pleased. He pushes Nut up into the heavens to keep them apart. Either way there is now enough space for humans to live. Nut was however already pregnant, and she gives birth to 5 children: Osiris, great God of the Earth; Isis, the Queen of the Earth; Set (or Seth), the black sheep of the family - physically speaking I hasten to add – Horus; and Nephthys. Atum is pleased with Osiris, despite the fact that he marries his sister Isis, and leaves the world in his care. Osiris designs the world - i.e. Egypt - with an eye towards perfection: the beautiful river, a wonderful climate and abundant vegetation to answer all the needs of its people. In all things Osiris observes the single, most important principle of the Gods - that of harmony and order and balance in all things. This is known as "Ma'at".

Set became very jealous of Orsiris' success and power. He managed to obtain his exact measurements from his tailor and had a box made to those specifications. The box was beautifully carved and lavishly decorated, and was presented to specially invited guests at the next party. Set announced that the exquisite chest would be given to the one who would best fit inside it. When Osiris lay down in it, it was a perfect fit and Set slammed down the lid, secured it and dropped it in the middle of the Nile. Set announced that Osiris was dead and that he would now rule the world.

Isis was convinced that Osiris was still alive. She set out to find him, and she did, even though the chest that held the body of Osiris had drifted into the sea.

"A flood had cast it upon the land. It had lain in a thicket of young trees. A tree, growing, had lifted it up. The branches of the tree wrapped themselves around it; the bark of the tree spread itself around it; at last the tree grew there, covering the chest with its bark."

The land was Byblos and the tree produced a wonderful fragrance. The King and Queen of Byblos had the tree cut down and incorporated in a column of their palace. Isis approached them and the King had the column taken down and split open, revealing the chest. The royal couple supplied a ship and Isis, "never stirring from beside the chest" returned to Egypt where she hid it. Leaving Nepthys to guard it, Isis set out on a second journey to seek the herbs and other ingredients that would enable her to make the potion that would return Osiris to life. Set realized that Isis had found the chest and he immediately set forth to find out where it was hidden. Nepthys eventually gave up the secret, and when Set retrieved the chest he carved Orsiris' body into forty two (some say fourteen) pieces and scattered them over the length and breadth of Egypt.

Isis wept so bitterly when she returned and Nepthys told her what had happened. Isis set out, yet again, this time to gather together all the parts of her beloved Osiris. To assuage her guilt, Nepthys undertook the journey with her. Wherever they found a body part, they would perform funerary rites and bury the part, building a shrine which would protect it from Set. This is how Egypt was divided into forty two administrative parts or "nomes". The only body part that was not restored was the penis, which had been eaten by a fish.

"Isis then created a replacement part for the phallus and mated with her husband, becoming pregnant with her son Horus."

Orsiris was brought back to life. He became the God of the Underworld and the wise and righteous judge of the dead. Isis gave birth to her son Horus (known as Horus the Younger), who was brought up in secret. When he grew to manhood he did battle with his uncle Set to avenge his father. The war lasted eighty years, but Horus triumphed in the end; Set was ousted, although he managed to keep control of the deserts. One version of this myth tells the story of the last epic battle where Set, who was a shape-shifter, transformed himself into a rhinoceros as the armies met. Horus was not fooled and he threw his weapon, (curiously enough referred to as a "harpoon") which pierced deeply into the rhino's scull, killing Set. Horus and his mother Isis, ruled the earth together and wisely; in this way "Ma'at", harmony and balance, were restored to the land.

"I am the Son of Maat, and wrong is what I execrate.

I am the Victorious one."

Book of the Dead

In this story, as in all the mythology of Egypt, the concept of Ma'at is the primary good, i.e. harmony and balance.

Chapter Four

The Pantheon Of Gods

In order to facilitate discussion of Egyptian religion and mythology, an explanation of the concept of syncretism will be necessary. By definition, syncretism revolves around the concept of the union (or attempted fusion) of different systems of thought or belief (especially in religion or philosophy). Its use in Egyptian mythology applies to the shifting identities of the various Gods and the combinations and borrowings of attributes from one another to create a more appropriate deity. An example of this is the existence of Amun-Ra - a combination of Sky God with Sun God or, in another setting, Ra- Atum, which was a combination of Sun God with Creator God. Another characteristic in Egyptian mythology is the close link between certain gods and specific animals. The connection was often reflected in how the god was represented – usually a human body with an animal head. This form of worship was particularly popular during the Pre-dynastic and Late Dynastic periods. For example: Bastet was originally a lioness and then became a cat; as the Goddess of the Home, she is often shown with a cat's head and holding a "sistrum" which was a sacred rattle. Often there is a kindle of kittens by her side. Thoth, the God of Learning, Magic and Wisdom, is usually depicted with the head of an Ibis and carrying a pen and ink holder.

Ra (Re), the Sun God

One of the most important and beloved Gods. He caused the sun to rise each day and was often seen as the creator of the universe. He had three main aspects as he travelled through the sky in his sunship: Khepri, in the morning; Horakhty at midday and Atem in the afternoon. At night, he travelled through the Underworld. He "died" at the 5th hour, was united with Osiris and "re-born" at the twelfth hour, manifesting as Khepri, as the sun rose. He often fought grueling battles in the night, especially with Apophis, the Demon Snake. There was a strange bond between these two arch-enemies. Some ancient stories say that Apophis was actually Ra's umbilical cord. The Snake would drink the waters of Heaven, creating sandbank obstacles for Ra to navigate. Ra was depicted as a man with a hawk or falcon's head, crowned with a brilliant sun disc that was sometimes encircled by a sacred cobra. His cult was at its height during the New Kingdom.

"How beautiful is your rising on the horizon,
when you bring dawn to the earth by your radiance.
All the gods rejoice when they see you as king of
heaven."

The Papyrus of Ani

Osiris, God of the Underworld (Duart) and Death

His cult started in the 2nd dynasty and grew strongly, reaching its height in the Middle Kingdom. Having established Egypt, he travelled through the country, teaching life skills, agriculture and how to worship the gods to the people. He left his beloved sister/wife Isis in charge and continued his teaching around the world. He was said to have been born in Thebes, but other myths say he was the city's founder. He was trapped and finally killed by his jealous brother Set, after which he became the beloved lord of the Underworld. This was a fertile and gentle land where all the "righteous dead" lived. He was the judge you faced when you died. There were many festivals in his honor. He was normally depicted as a bearded, mummified human wearing a white, conical crown, trimmed with red ostrich feathers, and surmounted by a small golden disc. He carried a flail and a crook, which was the icon representing divine authority. He often has a green skin indicating his power over vegetation and an ability to resurrect himself. His cult temple is in Abydos where ancient Egyptians believed he was buried.

*"Hail to thee, author of the gods, King of North and
South, Osiris,
the triumphant one, possessing the entire universe in
his
beneficent alternations ; He is the Lord of the Universe
;
Grant me passage in peace. I am righteous, I speak not
falsehood
knowingly, I am not guilty of duplicity."*

Book of the Dead

Isis, Mother of Egypt, Goddess of the Moon, Nature and Fertility

She is closely associated with healing and medicine. She resurrected her husband/brother and healed her son. She was married to her brother Osiris and their love for each other was passionate and enduring; incest was acceptable in many ancient cultures and was seen as a way of maintaining pure, sacred bloodlines. She is often depicted with an empty throne as a headdress, representing the fact that Osiris, who should have been the ruler, was missing. Otherwise her headdress consists of a pair of cow horns encircling a lunar or solar disc. Sometimes she is painted in a yellow hue which is indicative of the indoor life; she is also frequently shown with the beautiful, outspread wings of a kite hawk or a kestrel. One of her icons is a sycamore tree and she is often seen holding her last born child

Horus the Younger in her arms. This image is considered to be a forerunner of the pictures of Mary holding the Christ child as her cult remained popular through the 6th century CE. She was warm and compassionate and a beloved goddess of families.

"She who gives birth to heaven and earth,
knows the orphan, knows the widow,
seeks justice for the poor, and shelter for the weak"

Book of the Dead

Set, or Seth, the God of Chaos, Hostility and later on, of Evil

He also held sway over clouds and storms and was associated with the plague. Set had many names: Seth, Seti, Sutech, Setech, Sutech. He was a very complex god and was different from the others in that originally he was regarded as troublesome rather than evil. This changed somewhat after his jealousy of Osiris caused him to kidnap and then kill him and usurp his throne. When Osiris' son, Horus the Younger, set out to avenge his father, the war raged for eighty years – a period in which Set lost part of his leg and his testicles. During this time there was great conflict between the Priests of Horus and the adherents of Set.

Yet it was Set who sat in the prow of Ra's sunboat during his nightly Underworld journeys and fought furious battles with the evil serpent of chaos, Apophis so that the sun might rise the next morning. The idea of duality was an important part of Egyptian mythological belief and the cult of Set stood in strong contrast to the cults of Osiris, Horus and Ra. The pharaohs reluctantly respected him because they regarded him as very powerful.

Set was depicted as a human with a nearly indescribable head. It looked like an aardvark and always shows a curved snout, while the ears are erect and squared off. He often has a forked tail. This was called the Set Animal. Sometimes he was depicted as a greyhound. His sacred animals were many: oryx, antelope, ass, boar, hippopotamus and crocodile. He was often shown in red, holding an "ankh", a cross with a loop above the transverse bar, representing "life" in one hand and a "was" staff in the other. The "was" staff or sceptre was a long stick with a two pronged base and a transverse, angled top, often shaped like a bird or a "Set animal". It was a symbol of authority. During the New Kingdom his cult temple was at Ombos.

At one stage Set was even expelled from Egypt by the other Gods. During his exile he was referred to as Set, the Abominable. By the 2nd Intermediate Period he was closely associated with the Hyskos invaders and subsequent rulers. During this time his cult temple was at Avaris and his consorts were the Hyskos Goddesses Anat and Astarte.

Horus, God of Light, also called God of Kings

"From the very earliest of times, the falcon seems to have been worshipped in Egypt as representative of the greatest cosmic powers. Many falcon gods existed throughout Egypt, though over time, a good number of these assimilated to Horus, the most important of the avian deities. Yet, from all his of many forms, it is nearly impossible to distinguish the "true" Horus. Horus is mostly a general term for a great number of falcon deities." (Dunn, J. See: http://www.touregypt.net/featurestories/horus.htm#ixzz4 0nyb4xIv)

A most ubiquitous God, he was always depicted either as a falcon, or a man with a falcon head surmounted by a sun disc. The speckled feathers were the stars of heaven and the beating of his wings created the gentle winds. Although he was also a sun god and referred to as the "God of the east," Horus and his link with the sky has more to do with his avian appearance than the sun. He was variously known as; "lord of the sky", "the one on high" and "Horus of the two horizons". In all his forms he has strong associations with light and the power of the sun. In fact his one eye represented the sun while his other the moon. Depending on the source one is using, the sun is the right eye and the moon the left – or the other way around. What is consistent is that in the long battle Horus had with Set to avenge his father's death and reclaim the throne of Egypt, Set clawed out Horus' moon eye and tore it into pieces. The eye was recovered and put together again by the God Thoth, who returned it to Horus; it became the symbol of a "state of soundness". This is known as the "wedjat" or "udjat eye" meaning "the eye that is well". The reigning king of Egypt was regarded as the incarnation of Horus.

Thoth, God of Wisdom, Learning, Arts, Magic and Scribe to the Gods.

Thoth also manifested under many names; Tehuty, Djehuty, Tetu and Zehuti to name a few. His cult temple was in the Delta at Hermopolis. As the power of his cult grew, some myths were re-written to proclaim him as the creator God. In the guise of the great Ibis, he was supposed to have laid the egg from which Ra was born. Some say he created himself through the power of his tongue. This is a ghostly presentiment of the beautiful opening of St. John's gospel in the Bible; "In the beginning was the word, and the Word was with God and God was the Word." Thoth is credited with being the inventor of hieroglyphics, arithmetic and astrology, and is usually depicted as carrying a pen and ink or a stylus and palette. He almost always has the head of an Ibis surmounted by the lunar crescent. His other sacred animal is the baboon, a shape he often assumes as well. He is a lunar deity and is called "he who balances"; a reference to his role as the record keeper in the Underworld when the deceased are judged by Osiris. He is known as the epitome of justice, the "Lord of Time" and the "Accountant of the Years". His wife, Seshat, assumes the duties of Ma'at at the judging of the deceased.

There is an air of mystery about him as he is considered to be the author of a book containing "all the secrets of the universe". Owning this book would make the possessor the most powerful sorcerer in the universe. It is called The Book of Thoth or the "emerald tablets of Thoth" and it is said to be hidden in a secret chamber near the Great Pyramid. One of the secrets it will supposedly reveal is that it will prove prove all the gods come from the lost city of Atlantis. Debate about whether these tablets really exist still rages to this day.

Chapter Five

Mythology In Day To Day Ancient Egypt

As a strong example of polytheism, there were about 2,000 gods available for worship in Egypt. Religion guided every aspect of everyday life, from the routine of the Pharaoh down to the laborer working in the fields. The belief was that the only thing that stood between human beings and the total chaos of the universe was the power and goodwill of the gods, who were able to control everything. If the gods were happy the sun would rise, the Nile would flow and the inundation would take place once a year, the crops would flourish and harvests would be fruitful, the seasons would follow one another in an orderly fashion, and there would be peace in the land. Ma'at would prevail; there would be balance and harmony. The rules of societal living were strict and clear.

- The Pharaoh was the absolute Monarch. He was a god or a human or both.
- The King was the head of Government and the military force, and was an incarnation of Horus.
- The Vizier was second in command and administrator of land surveys, the Treasury and building projects. He was also in charge of the Archives.
- There were forty two administrative regions called "nomes", all controlled by governors known as Nomarchs.

However, he real seat of power was the temple. The temples were controlled by the priests, and were were also "the backbone of the economy," as the priests supervised the granaries and were responsible for the collecting and storing of the harvests. They also held the treasures, artifacts and records of the local population.

Priests mostly came from the nobility and they were often professionals as well as officials of the temples. These were the physicians, engineers, architects and teachers who instructed others at the temple's university or school, which was called "The House of Life". Most priests would undertake regular periods as serving priests at the temple. There were four groups, or phyles, of priests. Each group worked three times a year on a one month rotation. Additionally, there were two classes of priests, the first known as "God's servants or prophets", who officiated in the presence of the their god's image and were empowered to interpret the oracles' messages. These "pure ones" carried their god's barque, poured water libations and produced the sacred objects of the cult. For some devotees it would become a full time calling. Next was what was sometimes called the "white kilt class" in recognition of the fact that most of them dressed in unbleached linen. This was an "upper class" consisting of scribes and officials.

However, the bulk of the Egyptian population consisted of farmers, with a good sprinkling of craftsmen and artists among them. Everyone and everything was focused on appeasing the gods and following precise rituals to please, satisfy and glorify the pantheon as a whole. Generally speaking, the gods were considered well disposed and fair but, with having so many, the changing myths, syncretisms, and outside influences of foreign gods during periods of war and occupations, would lead to their demands being overwhelming at times. However, the various and complex ideas were never questioned or even considered contradictory by the general population. Instead they were simply regarded as "layers in the multiple facets of reality" as one Egyptologist has put it. There was usually a central temple in a large town, with several smaller ones as well, each dedicated to a particular main deity but also housing minor deities. Yet every little town, or even a temporary settlement, would have a temple at its center where certain rituals would be followed every day. See Temple Rituals below.

From a theological standpoint, all humans were deemed equal before the law. A human being was made up of discrete "aspects". It is difficult to relate to these aspects – not so much the because of the language but the functions of the aspects; we understand the make-up of a human being very differently today. To the Egyptians, the physical body was khat and had a twin named ka which was an immortal life-force, or the will. The main aspect of the body was the heart, and was considered the seat of emotion, intelligence and moral sense. When the heart was tired the body died and the ka departed to its spiritual origin. The next aspect was the name, which was vitally important as the very foundation of the being. You could not exist without a name, for it was your essence. It is why one might have several names, with each one to match one of the different aspects of your being. Ra had over a hundred different names according to The Book of the Dead; additionally, "he lives whose name is spoken" is an old Egyptian proverb.

Additionally, every body had a "shadow" but it is not clear what purpose it served. It could move independently of the body and did not have to remain in the grave. The next aspect was the ba; it is explained as "the sum of the immortal forces inherent in human beings which made up his personality." Today we might perhaps characterize the ba as the psyche. The final aspect is the akh. This comes into being when the ba and the ka re-unite; at that point, the akh manifests as the "Shining One" and takes its place as a star in the sky.

There is another version of what happens after death, which involves the soul needing to make a difficult journey through the Underworld until it reaches the Hall of Truth. Here the deceased will be judged by Osiris with Horus, Anubis and Thoth at hand, to see if they qualify to live forever in the beautiful Fields of Reeds, where they will enjoy a happier version of life on earth where there is no sickness, no disappointments and no death. This is one of the truly attractive aspects of Egyptian mythology; one is not expected to have led a perfect life. Instead, a balanced life is what is required in line with the expectations of Ma'at; harmony, order, justice, proper conduct. After reciting the forty two negative confessions of all the dreadful things that you have not done, your heart will be weighed on a golden scale against the weight of a white feather to judge how you have spent your time on earth. If your heart is lighter you will go to the Fields of the Reeds. If you fail and your heart is heavier, it will fall off the scale to the floor and be devoured by Ammit, the God with the face of a crocodile, the front of a leopard and the back of a hippopotamus, and your soul will cease to exist. In Egyptian Mythology, there is no hell as a place of torment.

The White Feather

"Given.
Many fear death
Because they already
Feel ridden with sin,
But no man on this earth
Is filled with only white light
Within.
Have more faith
In our Maker,
For our souls and minds
Were created by Him.
Just remember that,
When your deeds
Are measured
By the scale –
The good side
Must outweigh
The bad,
And your heart
Must be as light
As a feather
To win."

Suzy Kassem from Rise Up and Salute the Sun.

Chapter Six

The Central Role Of The Temple And Some Temple Rituals

A temple was consecrated to the central god of the town or village and the god was made accessible in the form of a large image that was kept in a sacred chamber of the temple. All temple rituals were aimed at "maintaining the fabric and process of the universe", and some had to take place at every temple, three times every day. Remember that during the night, Osiris travelled through the Underworld in his barque, frequently in battle with evil forces like Apophis, to ensure that Ra (the sun) would rise, bringing the next day. At every temple, every day, as the sun rose, the priests and assistants would have to bathe, dress and feed the main god and then praise him, thanking him for the new day. Most temples also housed lesser deities as well, and their needs also had to be taken care off. It is important to note that the image of the god was not worshipped. The image was simply a receptacle for the God's ka which was honoured. The daybreak ritual was elaborate, and the priests and other staff would be at the temple long before dawn to prepare a large and substantial first meal for the god. This might include meat, bread, beer, cakes, honey, fruit and vegetables. A small portion is set aside for the god and offered to him as part of the ritual. The rest is divided up between the temple staff once the morning ritual is complete, which often included the following actions:

o   A fire would be lit and incense burned in the public forecourt of the temple. The temple choir might sing hymns in honor of the god.

o   The priests proceed to the sealed opening of the god's shrine.

o   Accompanied by hymns and burning incense the clay or mud seal was broken.

o   The cord around the doorknobs was untied.

o   The priest would call out, representing the king: "It is the king who has sent me to see the god."

o   Light from the rising sun is introduced to the face of the god

o   On "seeing" the god, the priest would kiss the ground, raise his arms while singing, and then prostate himself, stretching his arms out in front of him to lie on his stomach.

o   Gifts of incense, oil or honey are offered.

o   The previous day's offerings are removed.

o   The priest's hands are purified before he touches and bathes the god

o   The god is dressed in four new lengths of cloth; white; blue; green and then blue once more.

o   He is offered scented oil and his face is painted with green (copper) and black (lead) eye paint.

o   An offering, perhaps a small statue, personifying Ma'at and "What is Right" is offered.

o   A very small selection from the meal is placed before the image. The "essence" of the meal is what the god requires.

o   The priest withdraws from the shrine, moving backwards and erasing his footprints as he goes.

o   Offerings of natron, incense and fresh water are left behind.

o   The chamber is resealed and locked.

Each part of this ritual had specific words that had to be repeated every time the ritual is performed, although there were many versions of what is required. These were referred to as formulas. After the main god has been honored, variations of these duties were performed for the lesser gods who might have also been housed in the temple. These rituals had to be performed three times a day in every temple, no matter how big or small. It has been noted that the midday and sunset rituals were not usually so elaborate, but had to be performed nonetheless.

The ordinary people were not allowed access the inner sanctuary of the temple, so the priests had to devise other, meaningful ways to allow them access to their gods. To this end there was a calendar of religious festivals arranged for the year at the larger religious centers. The highlight of such a festival would be a parade of the priests carrying the god in a shrine through the streets on a specially prepared and gorgeously decorated barque.

These festivals were important and strengthened the link between the ordinary people and the gods. The ordinary person was also given the opportunity to consult the god as an Oracle at this time. Certain stops along the way would be selected where the barque would be set down and the god would be revealed. If you had a pressing problem you could write it down in the form of a question that could be answered by a "yes" or a "no" and present it to the priest, who would then present it to the god. The questions could be written on a flake of limestone called an ostraca, or rolled up on a small piece of papyrus and placed in something else, such as an amulet. "You would get your answer from the God who would move forwards or backwards depending on if the answer were "yes" or "no". The parade would be followed by a feast for the people supplied by the god. One of the largest such feasts on record lasted 27 days during which 3,694 loaves of bread, 410 cakes and 905 jars of beer were happily consumed! Of course there would also be less elaborate festivals at all the local villages along the Nile. Individuals would also have shrines or special places set aside for their favorite and domestic gods in their homes or gardens. Personal piety was regarded as very important; it seems from historical writings that have survived to this day that most Egyptians saw themselves living in a world with many dangers. In the New Kingdom, it became the fashion to build a special room at the rear of the formal temple for private prayer for ordinary citizens. They were rooms were aptly referred to as the "chapel of the Hearing Ear".

Chapter Seven

Sources Of The History Of Egyptian Mythology

Egyptian civilization is over 3,000 years old and the language is the second oldest in the world. Its origin is northern Afro-Asiatic and it is related to both the Berber and Semitic languages. It was written in the form of logograms (where a picture stood for a word) called hieroglyphics. The first example of hieroglyphics was discovered in a pre-dynastic tomb in Abydos and date from about 3200 BCE.

Formal script was used mainly on monuments like the pyramids and made exclusive use of hieroglyphics. This form of writing took a long time to produce and required knowledge and skill. A simpler, cursive form called hieratic and more suitable for writing on papyrus evolved for religious texts and routine record keeping. This was followed by the even more simplified demotic style in the 7th century BCE, used for business and literary texts.

Most of what we have pieced together of the mythology of Egypt comes from the extensive writings inside the passages and burial chambers of the discovered pyramids. Collectively they are known as the Pyramid and Coffin texts. This collection was started in 1881 (or 1880 depending on what source you consult) when Gaston Maspero discovered the Pyramid of King Unas from the 5th dynasty. These examples were all hieroglyphic funerary texts and also what seemed like autobiographical notes. In the early 19th century a papyrus written by an author known only as Ipuwer was found describing a period in Egyptian history that might well have been the time of the plagues and the biblical Exodus. There is an astonishing website which documents Egyptian historical findings over time, the latest ones being in February 2016. It can be found at: http://www.crystalinks.com/egyptnews.html

The Rosetta Stone

Despite the plethora of texts available, progress on translating Egyptian hieroglyphs was painfully slow thanks to the difficulty of deciphering the texts. This obstacle vanished with the discovery of the Rosetta Stone, which "changed everything" to use a popular phrase. It was a black basalt stone first found by Lieutenant Pierre-François Bouchard, an officer in Napoleon's invasion force, among the ruins of Fort St. Julion at the mouth of the Nile in 1799. The stone was turned over to Britain when Napoleon was defeated and Alexandria capitulated in 1801. This stone has one text on it, repeated in three different scripts: once in hieroglyphics (14 lines); once in demotic (32 lines) and once in Greek (54 lines). It was like a key to unlock the meaning of the hieroglyphics.

Scholars immediately set their sights on breaking the hieroglyphic code. This honor finally went to Jean-Francois Champollion (1790-1832) in 1822. The content of the Rosetta Stone itself was not very exciting, as it turned out to be a decree issued by a panel of priests assembled in honour of Pharaoh Ptolemy V Epiphanes, King of Egypt, in 195 BCE. It is the forerunner of an "annual report" and stones like this would have been displayed in the open forecourt of the local temple as a "report back" to the constituents. It enumerated events during his reign: taxes collected; privileges extended; an exceptional Nile inundation in the 8th year of his reign and subsequent planning for a dam; generous gifts to certain temples and grateful subjects demanding a statue be erected in his honor with the following plaque: "Ptolemy, the Savior of Egypt".

The Book of the Dead

The single most informative source of Egyptian mythology and mysticism we have is a collection of texts and spells in the so-called "Book of the Dead". This is a selection of formulae for securing eternal life for the elite of Egyptian society through specific burial practices. Most of these instructions date from the New Kingdom to the end of the Ptolemaic period. Copies have been found in various versions, with the first existing in five copies, inscribed in hieroglyphics on the walls and passages of the pyramids of kings at Sakkâra and in tomb inscriptions, sarcophagi, coffins, stelae and papyri from c2133 BCE to 200 CE. These were edited by the priests of the College of Annu. A second copy on papyrus and in hieroglyphics is known as the Theban version, and was much used during the 18th to the 20th dynasty. A third, very similar version is also on papyrus, written in hieroglyphics and hieratic script, and was in use in the 20th dynasty. The fourth version, known as the Saïte version, is also in hieroglyphs and hieratic script, and was used from the 26th dynasty till the end of the Ptolemaic period. A complete copy of The Book of the Dead can be found online at: https://archive.org/stream/egyptianbookofde00reno/egyp tianbookofde00reno_djvu.txt

The Shabaka Stone

Another source of information, though somewhat at odds with traditional thought at the time, is the Shabaka Stone. It is green breccia basalt stone, approximately 137 x 93cm, kept at the British Museum, but of unknown provenance. It is named after the Kushite Pharaoh Shabaka, who had discovered a worm-eaten papyrus found while inspecting an old temple in c716 – 702 BCE, and had its contents copied onto the stone. It has three sections: the first is known as the Memphis Theogany and is an alternative version of the creation of the world. It explains that the God Ptah brought the world into being through his heart and his words, much like the Christian God in the biblical Genesis. The second story concerns the long war between Horus and Seth which is brought to an end by mutual peacemaking - not by a great battle in which Horus defeats Seth.

*"Reed and papyrus were placed on the double door of
the House of Ptah.
That means Horus and Seth, pacified and united. They
fraternized so as to cease quarrelling
in whatever place they might be, being united in the
House of Ptah,
the "Balance of the Two Lands" in which Upper and
Lower Egypt had been weighed."*

From the Shabaka Stone.

The third story is about Osiris' body being washed out
on the shore of Memphis and his body having been buried
there rather than in the traditional Abydos.

Chapter Eight

The Underworld And Life After Death

There were always elaborate burial customs among the Pharaohs and the upper classes in Egypt. The poor however were usually buried in the desert where their remains were well preserved due to the prevailing dry weather conditions. The rich were usually buried in stone tombs, called mastaba, and the gods of course in their temples. It was the excellent condition of the skeletons retrieved from the desert that spawned the idea of mummification which reached its height in the New Kingdom. The Egyptians did not see death as finality but rather an interruption of life in this world in preparation for a happier life in the underworld. When the khat died the ka departed, leaving the ba and body behind. The body had to be preserved because eventually the ka would return to unite with the ba so that the akh could start its journey to the underworld. For this reason the person was buried with certain necessities: food; drink; clothing; some valued objects; some amulets or ornaments, sometimes even with a little barque for transport and often with little wooden figures called ushabty. Ushabty literally means "answerers"; they would take care of any duties that the deceased person might have to undertake in the Underworld. Of course there would also be many formulae buried with the travellers, carved on stone or written on papyri to ensure a safe journey.

The priests would perform the embalming and mummification. The process took 70 days. The internal organs were taken out of the lower left side of the body. Some descriptions say the heart was never removed and some indicate that only part of the heart was taken out, the rest was left in situ. The brain was extracted through the nose using a long bronze hook. The body and organs would all be desiccated by lying in a salt mixture called natron. Thereafter the organs would be sealed into canopic jars. The rest of the body would be treated with spices and perfumes. A heart scarab would be inserted next to what remained of the heart and then the body would be carefully wrapped in bandages of flaxen cloth. Formulae, prayers, charms and personal possessions might be placed next to the skin or in the folds of the bandages and the bandaged body would be smeared with gum. The body would be laid in a sarcophagus and be taken to the final resting place on a sled in a procession. On reaching the grave, the priest would perform a ritual called "opening the mouth" which would supposedly reanimate the mummy and send it on its way through the Underworld. The tomb would then be sealed. Initially the jars containing the body parts would be placed close to the mummy but, by the 21st dynasty the body parts were reinserted in the body before it was wrapped.

Chapter Nine

Pyramids And Their Locations

The pyramids are the largest physical remnants we have of any ancient civilization, the easiest to explain, yet the most difficult to understand. It's obvious that they are the final resting places of highly important individuals, but the mysteries of their construction – and how they were aligned so precisely with the aid of astronomy – leave us with more questions than answers. Like anything the Egyptians did, there were many rituals surrounding the building of a pyramid tomb. The first ritual, dating back to the 2nd dynasty, was called "stretching the cord" and it was done at night. The building was precisely aligned by careful astronomical observations. There are several ways in which this could have been done. A tool called a "market" or "merket" could have been used. This is a notched stick through which the Great Bear constellation could be viewed; this would have allowed architects to calculate true North, where a central maker was driven into the ground. The King would then stand opposite the Goddess Seshat, each holding a vertical pole linked together by a loop of rope. They would stretch out the rope and mark the four corners of the building by driving marker stakes into the ground. The priests would then hoe the foundation trench and mould a mud brick, which would sometimes be inscribed, and place it with any other "deposits" to be included in the foundation. A thin layer of Nile sand was poured into the trench and workmen would take over the task of filling the foundations. A large stone block would be placed in one corner at the start of the construction phase.

Once the construction was complete, the building had to be purified before it could be dedicated to the one who would be buried within. The purification ritual was called "the strewing of the besen" and would involve the spreading of gypsum or natron throughout the construction. The temple would then be dedicated to the particular god who would live or be buried there. This was always accompanied by one of the most important religious rituals: "the opening of the mouth". This ritual would allow the deceased to continue living in the Underworld. The mummy would first be purified using natron and cow's milk. The Kher heb, or priest conducting the ceremony, then performed the transmutation ritual which would turn the food offerings into spiritual food. He would then touch the mouth, eyes, ears and nose to awaken the senses and allow the deceased to partake of the essence of the food and drink which would be supplied regularly. Slits would be made in the bandages using the embalmer's tools: a ritual adze; a peseshkaf, which was a spooned blade and a sharper, serpent-headed blade. The entire ritual consisted of 75 episodes, accompanied by many spells or formulas, songs, flowers and the burning of sacred oils and incense. The sarcophagus or image would then be sealed in an inner chamber.

When scholars try to answer the question of why the pyramids have their triangular design and why they are so precisely located, the field becomes highly controversial. One romantic suggestion is that the apex of the structure would bring the person as close to the sky as possible. Why would that be so important? There are about 80 pyramids still standing in Egypt, and the most impressive are the three located at Giza, from the 4th dynasty. The largest was built by Pharaoh Khufu. Its base is 13 acres, is composed of 2,300,000 stone blocks and contains 3 burial chambers – and it is perfectly aligned with Orion and true North. It's also precisely 20 degrees Celsius inside. The cornerstones have an advanced ball and socket construction that deals effectively with heat expansion and earthquakes. There is an excellent video you will enjoy watching available online at: https://www.youtube.com/watch?v=rcKahraBiBY This sets out in detail the eight engineering feats that seem to be way beyond the skills of the Ancient Egyptians to scholars today. There are some aspects of the construction that these scholars say would be impossible to duplicate even today with our advanced technology.

Conclusion

The Egyptians did have extensive knowledge of the skies. This was how the priests were able to "predict" the inundation of the Nile. When they saw the star Sirius rise just before the sun, they knew the annual flood was imminent. This also became the marker for the Summer Solstice and the beginning of their new year. The statue of Isis at Dendera was precisely oriented to the returning of Sirius so that at the first heliacal rising, the jewel placed on her forehead would catch the light and glitter. So many of the Egyptian structures were sighted and constructed in such a way that the first rays of the rising sun would touch the Image of the god, even where it was ensconced in an inner chamber. This was in celebration of Ra having made another successful night time journey through the Underworld, bringing another day and keeping their world safe against the return of chaos.

A Sphinx

"Close-Mouthed you sat five thousand years and never let out a whisper.
Processions came by, marchers, asking questions you answered with grey eyes never blinking, shut lips never talking.
Not one croak of anything you know has come from your cat crouch of ages.
I am one of those who know all you know and I keep my questions: I know the answers you hold."

Carl Sandburg

Made in the USA
Middletown, DE
13 December 2017